A Peaceful Superpower

The Movement
against War in Iraq

Special Edition

by David Cortright

A Project of the Fourth Freedom Forum
Goshen, Indiana

Published in the United States of America in 2004 by
the Fourth Freedom Forum
803 North Main Street
Goshen, Indiana 46528
www.fourthfreedom.org

A peaceful superpower : the movement against war in Iraq / David Cortright
    Special editon. The book, *A Peaceful Superpower: the Movement against War in Iraq,*
    is forthcoming.
    Special edition ISBN 1-931-710-13-9 (pbk. . alk paper)
        1. antiwar movement   2. nonviolent social change

Cortright, David 1946–

Printed and bound in the United States of America
    The paper used in this publication meets the
    requirements of the American National Standard for
    Permanence of Paper for Printed Library Materials
    Z39.48-1984.

Contents

David Cortright is a research fellow at the Joan B. Kroc Institute for International Peace Studies at the University of Notre Dame and president of the Fourth Freedom Forum. He is a founder of the Win Without War coalition and the former executive director of SANE. He is the author of a dozen books, including *Soldiers in Revolt: The American Military Today* (1975) and *Peace Works: The Citizen's Role in Ending the Cold War* (1993).

Acknowledgments

Like its subject, this book is a collective enterprise, the product of a wide collaboration among many colleagues.

My greatest debt is to Linda Gerber, research director at the Fourth Freedom Forum, who assisted me at every step in the preparation of this manuscript. She provided invaluable research assistance and prepared all the notes and citations. She edited the entire manuscript and offered numerous suggestions for improvement. She provided constant encouragement and support. I am also indebted to Jennifer Glick, publications director at the Forum, who designed the book cover and layout, collected and edited all the graphic material, and managed the production and distribution process. Ruth Miller, my executive assistant, transcribed portions of the manuscript and provided support for the editing, production, and distribution of the book. Alistair Millar, Forum vice president, offered valuable editorial advice and encouragement throughout the project.

The manuscript benefited enormously from review comments and skilled editing by a number of colleagues: Van Gosse, history professor at Franklin and Marshall College and former organizing director of Peace Action; George A. Lopez, director of policy studies and senior fellow at the Joan B. Kroc Institute for International Peace Studies at the University of Notre Dame; Kelly Burdick, student at Bard College; Lynn Erskine, former coordinator of the Win Without War coalition; Celeste Kennel Shank, student editor and activist at Goshen College; Leslie Cagan, co-chair of United for Peace and Justice; and Alistair Millar, vice president of the Fourth Freedom Forum. This project also received valuable comments and assistance from Duane Shank, Robert Greenwald, Susan Shaer, Gordon Clark, Art Silverman, Gary Ferdman, Gene Case, Melissa Daar, David Fenton, Erik Gustafson, and Karl Shelly. I am grateful to all those who were interviewed for the book and who agreed to share their recollections and insights about the movement.

Introduction

On February 15, 2003 in hundreds of cities across the world an estimated ten million people demonstrated against war on Iraq. It was the largest single day of antiwar protest in human history. More than a million people jammed the center of London, and huge throngs marched in Rome, Barcelona, Berlin, Madrid, Paris, Sydney, and hundreds of other cities. An estimated four hundred thousand braved bitter cold in New York, and tens of thousands demonstrated in San Francisco.[1] The people of the globe spoke out as never before in one unified voice against the planned invasion of Iraq. "The world says no to war," was the slogan and the reality.

The February 15 demonstrations were the high point of a vast and unprecedented mobilization of public opposition to war. The Iraq campaign "was the largest transnational antiwar movement that has ever taken place," according to social movement scholar Barbara Epstein.[2] In the course of just a few months, the movement in the United States reached levels of mobilization that, during the Vietnam era, took years to develop. The Iraq movement was more international in character than any previous antiwar campaign, as protests were coordinated throughout the world and activists understood themselves to be part of a truly global struggle.[3] The movement represented a convergence of antiwar and global justice efforts in a common campaign against military-corporate domination.[4] It was an expression of what scholar Stephen Gill has called "new . . . forms of global political agency."[5] The movement emerged from traditional peace and justice networks and relied extensively on the knowledge and resources of organizations and individuals with previous experience in antiwar action. The roots of the Iraq antiwar movement reached back to the struggle against the first Gulf War, and even further to the nuclear disarmament movement and nuclear freeze campaign, the Central America solidarity movement, the antiapartheid struggle, and the Vietnam antiwar movement.

I was an active participant in the Iraq antiwar movement, and in many previous peace and justice campaigns. I write as an engaged activist, one who was intimately involved in many of the activities described here. Mine is not a detached, ivory tower stance. I strive to uphold rigorous scholarly standards, and document the facts presented, but I bring a perspective. I believe in history from the bottom up, and have participated in movements that attempted to shape history in that way. When I was drafted for the Vietnam War I joined the GI peace movement, organizing petitions and protests while on active duty, and eventually filing a federal lawsuit against the army. I later wrote about that experience in *Soldiers in Revolt*. Throughout the late 1970s and 1980s I was executive director of SANE, the Committee for a Sane Nuclear Policy, and was deeply involved in the nuclear weapons freeze campaign, the Central America solidarity movement, and efforts to block the MX missile program and halt nuclear testing. I wrote about that experience in *Peace Works*. When the Bush administration threatened war against Iraq, I connected with old and new colleagues to attend the founding meeting of United for Peace and Justice and helped create the Win Without War coalition. I also worked with my partners at the Fourth Freedom Forum and the Joan B. Kroc Institute for International Peace Studies at the University of Notre Dame to produce a series of policy reports rebutting the case for war and presenting alternative options for countering Saddam Hussein.[6] For months, as the buildup to war intensified, I was constantly engaged in coordinating coalitions, planning actions, raising money, writing articles, publishing reports, participating in protests, and speaking to the media. Millions of others were similarly immersed in continuous antiwar activity. This is our story, offered as both testament to history and assessment of the movement's impact and relevance.

The Iraq antiwar movement involved religious communities, trade unions, students, women's organizations, environmentalists, academics, business executives, Hollywood artists, musicians, and many more. The movement was built largely through the Internet, which served as the primary tool for developing and disseminating strategies and actions, and which made it possible to mobilize huge numbers of people on short notice with limited resources. The movement utilized the mass media effectively to communicate its message. The war and the international opposition to it were dominant news stories throughout the world for months, and antiwar activists found themselves in the unaccustomed position of being the center of media attention. For the first time in history, observed writer Rebecca Solnit, the peace movement was portrayed in the media as "diverse, legitimate and representative," which was a "watershed victory" for the movement's representation and long-term prospects.[7]

The Iraq antiwar movement was relatively free of sectarian acrimony among left factions. Differences existed, to be sure, as several coalitions emerged to reflect varying political perspectives and organizing strategies, but the sharp political divisions that split the Vietnam antiwar movement did not appear. The movement developed and peaked in a very short period of time, about six months, which provided little opportunity for ideological discussion and debate. It was a "global movement without leaders," Solnit wrote.[8] Many brilliant spokespersons and organizers emerged, to be sure, but millions of people stepped forward on their own to oppose the war in countless creative ways. Activists shared a common sense of urgency in attempting to prevent the invasion. Most also shared a common analysis of the Iraq war as a dangerous manifestation of U.S. militarism. Defenders of the Bush administration's Iraq policy talked openly of empire, which helped antiwar critics see the war as imperialist—as a U.S. effort to gain geopolitical control over vital Iraqi oil supplies, and as part of a neoconservative and Likudnik agenda to make the region safe for U.S. and Israeli political-military interests. The stark political realities of this aggressive policy brought together a wide range of progressive constituencies in a shared movement to resist war. The administration's radical agenda also alarmed many mainstream Americans, who found themselves for the first time listening to and agreeing with the concerns of the peace movement.

A few days after the February 15 demonstrations, *New York Times* reporter Patrick Tyler conferred "superpower" status on the antiwar movement. The huge antiwar demonstrations were indications, wrote Tyler, of "two superpowers on the planet: the United States and world public opinion." The White House faced a "tenacious new adversary" which was generating massive opposition to the administration's war policy and had left the world's greatest military power virtually alone in the international community.[9] Antiwar commentators quickly adopted the phrase and proclaimed their movement "the other superpower." Author Jonathan Schell wrote in *The Nation* of the movement's "immense power" in winning the hearts and wills of the majority of the world's people.[10] Even UN Secretary-General Kofi Annan used the phrase in referring to antiwar opinion.[11] A new form of global social movement had emerged, an unprecedented expression of collective consciousness and action bound together through the Internet.[12]

How did this "superpower" exert its influence? What, if any, impact did the antiwar movement have on the policies of the Bush administration? This volume analyzes the emergence of the Iraq antiwar movement and traces the extraordinary scale of its development, concentrating on the months prior to and immediately after the beginning of war in March 2003. I provide an overview of different elements of the movement, concentrating on the Win Without War coalition, in which I was most actively involved. I examine the activities of the United for Peace and Justice coalition, consider the role of nonviolent civil disobedience, and discuss the reaction to war in the religious community, among women and people of color, in the labor movement, and in the military. I give special attention to two key dimensions of the movement— the role of Internet-based organizing, and the movement's strategies for framing and delivering its message. I conclude with some reflections on the movement's overall impact.

Notes

1. Estimates of the numbers of demonstrators and antiwar events are drawn from the website of United for Peace and Justice, the largest grassroots peace coalition in the United States. United for Peace and Justice, "The World Says No to War," 15 February 2003, <http://www.unitedforpeace.org/feb15.html> (accessed 24 November 2003). In San Francisco, police and organizers estimated the crowd at two hundred thousand, but a careful analysis by the *San Francisco Chronicle*, employing an innovative aerial observation method, put the crowd at approximately sixty-five thousand. See "Counting Crowds Using Aerial Photography to Estimate the Size of Sunday's Peace March in S.F.," *San Francisco Chronicle*, 21 February 2003, <http://sfgate.com/cgi-bin/article.cgi?f=/c/a/2003/02/21/MN20213.DTL> (accessed 15 December 2003). For newspaper accounts of the protests, see Angelique Chrisafis et al., "Threat of War: Millions Worldwide Rally for Peace," *Guardian* (London), 17 February 2003, 6; Glenn Frankel, "Millions Worldwide Protest Iraq War," *Washington Post*, 16 February 2003, A1; Alan Lowell, "1.5 Million Demonstrators in Cities Across Europe Oppose a War in Iraq," *New York Times*, 16 February 2003, A20.

2. Barbara Epstein, "Notes on the Antiwar Movement," *Monthly Review* 55, no. 3 (July–August 2003): 109.

3. Epstein, "Notes on the Antiwar Movement."

4. Mark LeVine, "The Peace Movement Plans for the Future," *Middle East Report* (July 2003), <http://www.merip.org/mero/interventions/levine_interv.html> (accessed 24 November 2003).

5. Stephen Gill, *Power and Resistance in the New World Order* (London: Palgrave, 2003), 218.

6. See the following joint reports of the Fourth Freedom Forum and the Joan B. Kroc Institute for International Peace Studies at the University of Notre Dame: *Sanctions, Inspections, and Containment: Viable Policy Options in Iraq*, Policy Brief F3 (Goshen, Ind.: Fourth Freedom Forum, June 2002); *Winning Without War: Sensible Security Options for Dealing With Iraq*, Policy Brief F5 (Goshen, Ind.: Fourth Freedom Forum, October 2002); *The Progress of UN Disarmament in Iraq: An Assessment Report*, Policy Brief F7 (Goshen, Ind.: Fourth Freedom Forum, January 2003); *Contested Case: Do the Facts Justify the Case for War in Iraq?* Policy Brief F8 (Goshen, Ind.: Fourth Freedom Forum, February 2003); *Grading Iraqi Compliance*, Policy Brief F10 (Goshen, Ind.: Fourth Freedom Forum, March 2003); and *Unproven: The Controversy over Justifying War in Iraq*, Policy Brief F12A (Goshen,

Ind.: Fourth Freedom Forum, June 2003), <http://www.fourthfreedom.org> (accessed 8 January 2004).

7. Rebecca Solnit, "Acts of Hope: Challenging Empire on the World Stage," *Orion* (20 May 2003), <http://www.oriononline.org/pages/oo/sidebars/Patriotism/index_SolnitPR.html> (accessed 24 November 2003).

8. Solnit, "Acts of Hope."

9. Patrick E. Tyler, "Threats and Responses: News Analysis; A New Power in the Streets," *New York Times*, 17 February 2003, A1.

10. Jonathan Schell, "The Other Superpower," *The Nation* (27 March 2003), <http://www.thenation.com/doc.mhtml?i=20030414&s=schell> (accessed 24 November 2003).

11. Jeoffrey Nunberg, "As Google Goes, So Goes the Nation," *New York Times*, 18 May 2003, Section 4, 4.

12. James F. Moore, "The Second Superpower Rears its Beautiful Head," Berkman Center for Internet and Society at Harvard Law School, 31 March 2003, <http://cyber.law.harvard.edu/people/jmoore/secondsuperpower.html> (accessed 21 November 2003).

Chapter One

A War Predetermined

The Iraq antiwar movement had enormous influence in shaping strong majorities of public opinion against war. Yet the movement was unable to achieve its overriding objective of preventing the attack on Iraq. The unavoidable fact, as Jonathan Schell poignantly observed, was that "the candles in windows did not stop the cruise missiles."[1] The antiwar campaign may have delayed the onset of war, as the Bush administration was forced to spend frustrating months seeking an elusive diplomatic consensus, but even that small success is debatable. If the movement bought time for diplomacy, it was only a matter of months at best. This meager result reflected not the weakness of the movement, but the failures of democracy in the U.S. and the U.K., where majorities of people opposed a war fought without UN support or international allies. It also reflected the Bush administration's determination to overthrow the government of Saddam Hussein regardless of public opinion. The administration simply disregarded the rising chorus of opposition in the United States and around the world. In retrospect it seems that no movement, however massive or powerful, could have succeeded in dissuading the president and his advisers from their obsession with armed regime change in Iraq.

Neoconservatives in Washington had argued for war against Iraq throughout the 1990s. In the last days of the first Bush administration, Paul Wolfowitz, then under secretary of defense for policy, circulated a classified draft of a defense guidance document asserting that the United States must be "postured to act independently when collective action cannot be orchestrated."[2] In the document, Wolfowitz outlined plans for military intervention in Iraq as an action necessary to assure "access to vital raw material, primarily Persian Gulf oil."[3] When excerpts of the draft document were published in the *New York Times* in March 1992, it embarrassed the administration as being too hawkish and was shelved.[4] Support for war against Iraq did not die, however, as military hard-liners continued to urge the overthrow of Saddam Hussein and a more assertive U.S. military strategy to reshape Iraq and the Middle East. An influential group known as the Project for a New American Century (PNAC) emerged in 1997 to give voice to these sentiments. It was led by William Kristol, publisher of the *Weekly Standard*, and included among its supporters Dick Cheney, Donald Rumsfeld, and other future leaders of the Bush administration. In January 1998 the group sent a letter to President Clinton that urged "removing Saddam Hussein and his regime from power." Among the signers were Rumsfeld, Wolfowitz, and future assistant secretary of state John Bolton.[5] In September 2000 the group published *Rebuilding America's Defenses*, a detailed plan for a new American strategy of global military dominance that presaged the Bush administration's blueprint for military preemption released in September 2002. Wolfowitz, Cheney, and other Iraq hawks returned to power as part of the Bush-Cheney administration in 2001. According to Paul O'Neill, Bush's first treasury secretary, the new administration began planning the forced removal of Saddam from its very first days.[6] The terror attacks later that year and the national numbing that followed created a climate where the neoconservatives could pursue their vision of preemptive unilateralism and the military overthrow of the Baghdad government.

Concrete discussion of war against Iraq began within hours of the September 11 terrorist attacks. *Washington Post* reporter Bob Woodward described in *Bush at War* how the president was transformed into a war leader by the tragedy of September 11, and almost immediately began to think of Iraq as a potential target of attack. "I believe Iraq was involved," Bush said a few days after the terrorist attacks. He decided against striking then, but told the Pentagon to get ready.[7] Secretary of Defense Rumsfeld needed no encouragement. Within hours of the attack he instructed aides to develop justifications for invading Iraq. CBS News quoted notes from an aide who participated in a Pentagon meeting the afternoon of September 11 in which Rumsfeld ordered his staff: "Best info fast. Judge whether good enough hit SH [Saddam Hussein] at same time. Not only UBL [Usama bin Laden]. Go massive. Sweep it all up. Things related and not."[8] Rumsfeld raised the question of attacking Iraq at a White House meeting of the National Security Council on September 12.[9] PNAC sent a letter to the White House on September 20 asserting "even if evidence does not link Iraq directly to the [September 11] attack, any strategy aiming at the eradication of terrorism and its sponsors must include a determined effort to remove Saddam Hussein from power."[10]

Preparations for the attack on Iraq began in earnest soon after the overthrow of the Taliban regime in Afghanistan. Bush speechwriter, David Frum, recounted in his memoir that he was told to come up with a justification for war against Iraq for Bush's State of the Union address in 2002.[11] An initial wave of articles about possible war in Iraq appeared at the end of 2001, and the public discussion intensified throughout 2002 as the Bush administration finalized its invasion plans. The first major rattling of the saber was Vice President Cheney's August 2002 speech to the American Legion, which evoked the image of the Iraqi regime as an imminent menace requiring a military response. President Bush formally kicked off the public campaign for war with his September 2002 address at the United Nations, which came on the first anniversary of the terrorist attacks. The president implied a link between the terrorist threat and Saddam Hussein (despite the lack of verified evidence of an operational connection between the Baghdad government and Al Qaeda) and demanded that Iraq yield to UN disarmament. Although Saddam Hussein unexpectedly conceded to the demand for renewed inspections, and generally cooperated with the UN monitors when they reentered the country in December, the Bush administration pressed ahead with a steady drumbeat for war. The buildup of an invasion force accelerated in the final months of 2002, as war became increasingly inevitable.

Premonitions

Like the administration's planning for war, the development of the antiwar movement began in the immediate aftermath of September 11. Alarmed by the president's declaration of a "war on terror," and fearing that the metaphor of war would be turned into reality, peace and human rights activists began to call for a different kind of response to the terrorist attacks. An open-ended "war" against terror was a formula for continuous military conflict, they warned. Instead of war they called for a "just and effective response," which became the name of a new website established by the Fourth Freedom Forum on behalf of a coalition of groups.[12] Within days of the attacks, religious leaders began to circulate a statement appealing for "sober restraint" and warning against indiscriminate retaliation that would cause more loss of innocent life. "Let us deny them [the terrorists] their victory by refusing to submit to a world created in their image," the declaration read. Initiated by Reverend Jim Wallis, founder of Sojourners, and Reverend Bob Edgar, former congressman and general secretary of the National Council of Churches, the statement was eventually signed by more than four thousand religious leaders and was published in the *New York Times* on November 19, 2001.

Religious and peace activists argued for a counterterrorism strategy based on cooperative law enforcement rather than unilateral military action. The terrorist attacks were a crime, they emphasized, not an act of war. The proper response was not military action, but a vigorous, multilateral police effort to apprehend the perpetrators and prevent future attacks. Activists also appealed for greater attention to the root causes of political extremism—not to excuse terrorism, but to understand and address the factors that motivate such violence. They called for greater efforts to heed the voice of the powerless and resolve the grievances of the oppressed. They proposed policies that could mitigate anti-American resentment and enhance global security: a reduced U.S. military presence in the Arab and Muslim world, support for a just peace in the Middle East, and funding for equitable development and poverty reduction efforts. The peace movement advocated these and other approaches as it struggled to frame its message in the radically altered post–September 11 political environment.

Many social justice activists feared that the government would use the September 11 tragedy not only as a pretext for war but also as an excuse to crack down on immigrants and people of color. In the San Francisco Bay area several veterans of racial justice campaigns decided to create a new publication, *War Times*, which they hoped would serve as a vehicle for outreach and consciousness raising for a new kind of peace and justice movement. The groups decided to test the public response to their concept by producing a pilot issue in January 2002. Bob Wing, managing editor of the new paper, described what happened:

> We put the prospectus up on the Internet and within a week we had seventy thousand orders. We had decided to jump off a cliff and see if anyone would give us a parachute. The response was overwhelming. It blew it open for us. We gave the paper away free, but donations kept coming in to keep the presses running.[13]

The monthly distribution soon reached 130,000. From the outset *War Times* was published in English and Spanish. The paper focused not only on the buildup toward war but the increasing harassment and pressures faced by immigrants and racial minorities. The paper became an important organizing tool for broadening the antiwar movement. Wing became a key player in the leadership of United for Peace and Justice.

On the day after September 11, Eli Pariser, a recent college graduate living near Boston, sent an e-mail message to a group of friends urging them to call for multilateral police action rather than war in response to the terrorist attacks.[14] Friends forwarded his message to others, and it began to spread exponentially. In the vernacular of the Internet, it went viral. At the same time, a recent graduate of the University of Chicago, David Pickering, posted a similar message on a campus website. When Pariser saw it, he contacted Pickering, and the two joined forces on a new website, 9-11peace.org. Within a week, 120,000 people from 190 countries had signed their petition against war. By the first week of October more than half a million signed. Pariser and his colleagues had discovered what a *New York Times* reporter later called "an organizing tool of dazzling power."[15] It was the beginning of Internet-based peace organizing on a mass scale. A few months later Pariser teamed up with Wes Boyd and Joan Blades, software entrepreneurs in California, who had created MoveOn in 1998 to stop the impeachment of Bill Clinton. With Pariser spearheading its international campaigns, MoveOn quickly emerged as a major organizational and financial power in the fledgling antiwar movement.

The September 11 attacks had an enormous impact on the global justice movement. The struggle against corporate globalization had burst dramatically onto the political stage with the huge protests and urban lockdowns in Seattle in November 1999, followed by similar actions in Washington, Prague, Quebec, and Genoa. Another action had been planned for September 2001 in Washington, but was cancelled after the terrorist strikes. The social trauma that followed in the immediate aftermath of the attacks was not conducive to continued protests. For a time the global justice movement suffered from a loss of direction, and was unable to recapture its previous momentum. Ironically, the war drive of the Bush administration gave the movement a new sense of urgency and purpose. Thousands of activists in the United States and around the world began to see, as one activist leader put it, that "militarization was just the other arm of the corporate agenda."[16] Many suspected, as events would later prove, that a U.S. takeover of Baghdad would lead to the attempted privatization of Iraq's economy and would open the door to corporate profiteering by politically connected U.S. firms. Global justice activists began to pour their energy and creativity into the emerging antiwar movement.

The response to the Bush administration's militarized policies also included traditional street protests. Demonstrations and rallies are a natural social response to government policies that endanger or offend the public interest. They are an essential means of drawing attention to a movement's grievances and demands. They help to build solidarity and commitment among activists. But they can also attract fringe groups, which may create divisiveness within the larger movement. This was a major dilemma during the Vietnam antiwar movement,[17] and similar though less severe problems emerged during the Iraq campaign. The first group to organize national protests against the war buildup was ANSWER (Act Now to Stop War and End Racism), a coalition formed by the splinter group, Workers World Party. ANSWER called for a demonstration in Washington on September 29, 2001 to oppose the Bush administration's war plans. The initial rally was relatively small, attracting about ten thousand demonstrators. ANSWER organized larger rallies in Washington on April 20 and October 26, 2002, and January 18, 2003. Other groups cosponsored these subsequent rallies, but ANSWER usually controlled the program. Speakers at the rallies condemned the war in Afghanistan and plans for the invasion of Iraq, but they also supported a variety of other causes, from freedom for Mumia Abu-Jamal to support for Palestinian rights. Many activists, myself included, attended the ANSWER rallies because of a desire to be counted in opposition to the Bush administration's policies, but we were turned off by the coalition's sectarianism. Veteran activist Todd Gitlin wrote a commentary for *Mother Jones* magazine in October 2002 decrying the "old left" tenor of the antiwar movement to date, and calling for an "extensive, inclusive popular movement" against the policies of the Bush administration.[18] "We don't like the Workers' World Party," said an activist from the Pittsburgh-based Thomas Merton Center during the October 2002 rally, "but they're the only game in town."[19] Many of us wanted to see a new game, and we yearned for a more diverse, broadly-based antiwar movement.

On the day before the April 20 ANSWER-sponsored mobilization in Washington, two dozen representatives from a range of religious and peace groups met to discuss the threat of war. I helped to organize the meeting, and Susan Shaer, executive director of Women's Action for New Directions (WAND), chaired the session. We discussed a number of possible action strategies but made no decisions and did not attempt to form a new coalition. Some activists later questioned why we had not been more decisive. If we had called for a new coalition then, perhaps the antiwar movement would have taken shape sooner, and we might have had a greater chance of actually stopping the war. At the time, however, it was difficult to predict when and if the war would begin. Many people still believed, or perhaps were trying to convince themselves, that the Bush administration was merely using threats and coercive diplomacy to pressure Saddam Hussein, that the White House didn't really intend to invade Iraq. I was convinced of the contrary, that the administration meant business and was intent on war, but it was often hard to persuade others. The sense of urgency that would come later was not yet present.

Congress Caves

During an early antiwar strategy meeting, several people suggested that demanding a congressional vote might be a way of preventing or delaying the march toward war. The assumption, naïve in retrospect, was that members of Congress would object to such an obviously unjustified attack. Be careful what you wish for, other activists cautioned. Don't count on Congress to challenge the president's war authority or stand in the way of military action. Congress might simply roll over and give the president whatever he wants. This pessimistic assessment was based on an accurate reading of U.S. history. Congress long ago abdicated its constitutional authority to declare war. For decades legislators have either stepped aside or actively cheered as the executive branch employed U.S. troops abroad and accumulated ever-greater authority to wage war. In 1964 Congress passed the infamous Gulf of Tonkin resolution, based on a nonexistent attack against U.S. naval forces, providing the president virtually unlimited authority to wage war in Indochina. Congress was particularly hawkish in its posture toward Iraq. In 1998 Congress approved the so-called Iraq Liberation Act, asserting that it should be the policy of the United States to support efforts to remove Saddam Hussein from office. That same year Congress urged the president to take "appropriate action . . . to bring Iraq into compliance" with its UN obligations.[20]

As the White House launched its public campaign for war in August and September 2002, the administration initially claimed that congressional approval was not necessary for an invasion of Iraq. White House lawyers drafted a legal brief asserting that the president could go to war without any further endorsement from Congress or the United Nations.[21] Congressional leaders objected to this interpretation. Republicans as well as Democrats expressed anxieties that Bush was leading the country to war without thinking through the implications or consulting allies. In early September the White House yielded to these concerns and announced that it would seek congressional approval. This touched off an intensive period of political jockeying in which Democrats and some moderate Republicans attempted to place limits on the president's war- making authority. Senators Joseph Biden (D-DE) and Richard Lugar (R-IN), leaders of the Senate Foreign Relations Committee, introduced legislation specifying that military force could be used only to disarm Iraqi weapons of mass destruction. Their measure would have required the president to win the approval of the UN Security Council before using force, or issue a determination that the threat to security was so grave that he needed to act without UN authorization. Senator Carl Levin (D-MI), chair of the Senate Armed Services Committee, proposed a measure that would have flatly prohibited military action without explicit Security Council approval. These and other efforts to limit the president's authority were undermined when House Minority Leader Richard Gephardt (D-MO) cut a deal with the White House in early October. The Bush-Gephardt compromise gave the president virtually unchecked authority to use military force, while offering the fig leaf of further consultations with Congress and the requirement of a presidential determination that diplomacy was no longer working.[22] Gephardt's action undercut Democratic efforts to restrain the president's war-making authority and handed the White House a major political victory. On October 10 Congress approved a joint resolution authorizing the president "to use the armed forces of the United States as he determines to be necessary and appropriate . . . against the continuing threat posed by Iraq." The vote in the Senate was 77–23, and in the House 296–133.[23]

Antiwar groups attempted to mobilize against the war resolution. MoveOn organized hundreds of antiwar meetings with members of Congress in local districts in August. The Friends Committee on National Legislation joined with Education for Peace in Iraq and other Washington-based groups to form an Iraq Working Group that lobbied members of Congress and coordinated grassroots constituency pressure. Members of Congress reported substantial voter unease about the prospect of war, and constituent messages reportedly ran four to one against the use of force.[24] A major demonstration in Washington might have helped to pressure Congress, but the ANSWER-sponsored rally came on October 26, two weeks after the congressional vote. The inability of the antiwar movement to prevent the White House from winning congressional authorization was a major blow to the prospects of stopping the invasion or limiting the scope of military action. The movement was not yet sufficiently large or well organized to wield the level of political clout that would have been necessary to block congressional approval.

As expected, most Republicans voted for the president's war authorization, but so did many Democrats, much to the disappointment of antiwar activists. Even erstwhile liberals such as John Kerry of Massachusetts and Hillary Rodham Clinton of New York voted for war. As their constituents were mobilizing for peace, these senators were scrambling for political cover. Kerry attempted to rationalize his vote by saying that it was not an explicit authorization for war but simply an endorsement of tough diplomacy. As a former leader of Vietnam Veterans Against the War during the early 1970s, Kerry should have known better. The Democrats who voted for the war resolution in October fell victim to a trap set by White House political adviser Karl Rove. The White House strategy for the November 2002 midterm elections was to focus on Iraq

Patterns of Congressional Opposition to War

Percentage of Indicated Group Voting No
on October 2002 Iraq War Resolution[25]

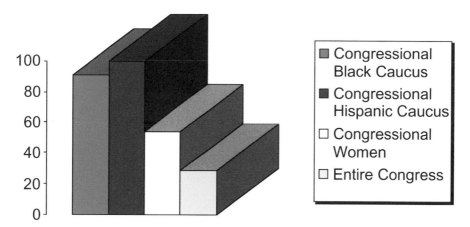

and the threat of terrorism, as a way of rallying voter support behind a wartime president, and taking advantage of higher Republican approval ratings on national security issues. For the White House, the war debate was a useful distraction from domestic economic issues and corporate malfeasance, where Republicans were politically vulnerable. Democrats hoped to get the war vote out of the way early in the campaign, so that the focus of public attention could swing back to Bush's unpopular domestic policies. The White House easily trumped this losing strategy, and Republicans won control of the Senate in the midterm elections. By standing aside on the vital issue of war, Democrats lost credibility and political standing.

The vote on the congressional war resolution revealed important cleavages in American political life. White male members of Congress from both parties voted overwhelmingly to endorse war. African-American, Latino, and women legislators, on the other hand, voted against the use of military force. Among the thirty-three voting members of the Congressional Black Caucus, thirty voted against the resolution. Every one of the sixteen members of the Hispanic Congressional Caucus who voted that day opposed the measure. Among the seventy female members of the Senate and House who participated in the vote, thirty-eight decided against the resolution. These votes in Congress reflected the greater skepticism about war among Blacks, Latinos, and women in the general population.

Notes

1. Jonathan Schell, "The Other Superpower," *The Nation* (27 March 2003), <http://www.thenation.com/doc.mhtml?i=20030414&s=schell> (accessed 24 November 2003).

2. Significant portions of the documents were printed in the *New York Times* and the *Washington Post*. See Patrick E. Tyler, "U.S. Strategy Plan Calls for Insuring No Rivals Develop A One-Superpower World: Pentagon's Document Outlines Ways to Thwart Challenges to Primacy of America," *New York Times,* 8 March 1992, and Barton Gellman, "Keeping the U.S. First; Pentagon Would Preclude a Rival Superpower," *Washington Post,* 11 March 1992, A1.

3. Joseph Cirincione, "Origins of Regime Change in Iraq," Carnegie Endowment for International Peace Proliferation Brief 6, no. 5 (2003), <http://www.ceip.org/files/Publications/originsofregimechangeiniraq.asp?p=8&from=pubdate> (accessed 24 November 2003).

4. Steven R. Weisman, "A New Doctrine; Pre-emption: Idea With a Lineage Whose Time Has Come," *New York Times,* 23 March 2003, B1. For more details on the changes that occurred from Donald Rumsfeld's first circulated draft to the version signed by Defense Secretary Dick Cheney, see Patrick Tyler, "Pentagon Drops Goal Of Blocking New Superpowers," *New York Times,* 23 May 1993, A1.

5. Project for a New American Century, "Letter to President Clinton on Iraq," 26 January 1998, <http://www.newamericancentury.org/iraqclintonletter.htm> (accessed 1 December 2003).

6. Ron Suskind, *The Price of Loyalty: George W. Bush, the White House, and the Education of Paul O'Neill* (New York: Simon and Schuster, 2004).

7. Bob Woodward, *Bush at War* (New York: Simon and Schuster, 2002), 99.

8. CBS, "Plans for Iraq Attack Began on 9/11," 5 September 2002, <http://www.cbsnews.com/stories/2002/09/04/september11/main520830.shtml> (accessed 24 November 2003).

9. Woodward, *Bush at War*, 49.

10. Project for a New American Century, "Letter to President Bush," 20 September 2001, <http://www.newamericancentury.org/Bushletter.htm> (accessed 1 December 2003).

11. John B. Judis and Spencer Ackerman, "The Selling of the Iraq War: The First Casualty," *The New Republic* (30 June 2003), <www.tnr.com/docprint.mhtml?i=20030630&s=ackermanjudis063003> (accessed 24 November 2003).

12. See the Just Response website, <http://www.justresponse.org> (accessed 1 December 2003).

13. Bob Wing, interview by author, 14 November 2003.

14. George Packer, "Smart-Mobbing the War," *New York Times Magazine*, 9 March 2003, 46.

15. Packer, "Smart-Mobbing the War."

16. Leslie Cagan, interview by author, 26 August 2003.

17. The Trotskyist Socialist Workers Party competed with groups in the Vietnam Mobilization Committee and sponsored its own coalition and separate mass rallies. For historical perspectives on the Vietnam movement, see Tom Wells, *The War Within: America's Battle Over Vietnam* (Berkeley: University of California Press, 1994) and Charles DeBenedetti, *An American Ordeal: The Antiwar Movement of the Vietnam War* (Syracuse: Syracuse University Press, 1990). For a Socialist Workers Party perspective, see Fred Halstead, *Out Now: A Participant's Account of the Movement in the United States against the Vietnam War* (New York: Monad Press, 1978).

18. Todd Gitlin, "Who Will Lead?" *Mother Jones* (14 October 2002), <http://www.motherjones.com/commentary/gitlin/2002/10/we_175_01.html> (accessed 24 November 2003).

19. David Corn, "Behind the Placards: The Odd and Troubling Origins of Today's Antiwar Movement," *LA Weekly*, 1–7 November 2002.

20. The 1998 congressional resolutions on Iraq are: Public Law 105-235, 105th Cong., 2d sess. (14 August 1998) [*Iraqi Liberation Act of 1998*]; and Public Law 105-338, 105th Cong., 2d sess. (31 October 1998) [*Iraqi Breach of International Obligations*].

21. Miles A. Pomper, "Bush Hopes to Avoid Battle with Congress over Iraq," *Congressional Quarterly Weekly* 60, no. 33 (31 August 2002): 2252.

22. Miles A. Pomper, "Senate Democrats in Disarray After Gephardt's Deal on Iraq," *Congressional Quarterly Weekly* 60, no. 38 (5 October 2002): 2606-07.

23. Jim VandeHei and Juliet Eilperin, "Congress Passes Iraq Resolution," *Washington Post*, 11 October 2002, A1.

24. Andrew Taylor, "Though Neither Party is Crying 'Politics,' Election Year Puts War Vote on Fast Track," *Congressional Quarterly Weekly* 60, no. 34 (7 September 2002): 2317; and Gebe Martinez, "Democratic Group Finds Tough Sell in Go-Slow Approach to War," *Congressional Quarterly Weekly* 60, no. 37 (28 September 2002): 2500. Reports of four to one constituent messages provided by Lynn Erskine, e-mail message to author, 22 December 2003.

25. Vote percentages against the war by group are as follows: Congressional Black Caucus—90 percent; Congressional Hispanic Caucus—100 percent; Congressional women—54 percent; and the entire Congress—29 percent. Research gathered from publicly available voting records and caucus membership rolls.

Chapter Two

Uniting
for Peace and Justice

As the administration made its bellicose intentions clear in August and September 2002, the need for more effective antiwar leadership intensified. A growing number of activists began to call for a more broadly based national effort to oppose war in Iraq. In August I wrote an article for *The Progressive* magazine, "Stop the War before it Starts," arguing for a mainstream movement that could "capture the patriotic wave" and build broad public opposition to war. During the summer several experienced peace and justice activists began a series of discussions with the specific goal of forming a new coalition. One of the most important figures in this effort was Bill Fletcher, president of TransAfrica Forum. Fletcher was a veteran of twenty-five years in the labor movement and the former education director and assistant to the president of the AFL-CIO. Fletcher worked with Van Gosse, former organizing director for Peace Action, to contact a range of peace and justice activists about the prospects for creating a unified antiwar coalition.[1] Gradually an initial planning group came together to call for a public meeting. On October 25, 2002, the day before the ANSWER-sponsored rally in Washington, representatives of more than fifty peace, religious, and social justice organizations gathered in Washington to address the threat of war. The meeting was co-chaired by Fletcher and Leslie Cagan, a veteran organizer widely respected throughout the peace movement.[2] The breadth of participation in the meeting reflected the wide recognition that an effective antiwar coalition was urgently needed. Cagan described the moment and the process:

> The Bush administration's push toward war, and the growing
> opposition to it . . . led a number of people to feel that we should
> try to put together something that would have a broader reach,
> that would not just mobilize the most obvious layer of
> discontent, but would try to bring into play much broader forces.
> So people who knew each other from previous antiwar, anti-
> intervention, nuclear disarmament, and general foreign policy
> activism started talking to each other. An initial group of about

ten to twelve people gathered in Washington in early October and agreed to organize a larger meeting on October 25.[3]

Participants in the larger meeting included traditional peace organizations that had led previous antiwar efforts (Peace Action, American Friends Service Committee, Women's Action for New Directions [WAND], Sojourners, War Resisters League, Fellowship of Reconciliation); representatives of the new Internet-based groups (MoveOn and True Majority, an activist network founded by ice cream entrepreneur Ben Cohen); global justice groups such as Global Exchange; and major constituency organizations (National Organization for Women, the Rainbow/PUSH Coalition, and the Center for Community Change). The meeting lasted all day, as nearly every one of the approximately ninety participants took a turn at speaking and debating a wide range of issues and action strategies. At the end of the session, participants agreed to create a new antiwar coalition, taking its name, "United for Peace," from a website of the same name created by Global Exchange. Cagan, Fletcher, and Andrea Buffa of Global Exchange were asked to chair the new coalition, and an ad hoc committee was selected to work out the details of process and program that were left unresolved.

The new coalition faced multiple challenges as it struggled to take shape: an imminent war threat, a lack of financial and organizational resources, and an unwieldy participatory process that complicated the task of deciding structure and strategy. One of the coalition's early decisions was to change its name to "United for Peace and Justice," which reflected a desire to link the cause of peace to the struggle for racial and economic justice. For the first two months the coalition operated without staff or office space. Cagan served as unpaid, indispensable coordinator, while participating groups—Global Exchange, Institute for Policy Studies, Peace Action, Democracy Rising, and others—contributed staff and resources.[4] Office space was finally secured in January, donated by 1199 Service Employees' International Union, New York's Health Care Union.

United for Peace and Justice was quintessentially a grassroots activist coalition, and its principal action strategy was to organize protest demonstrations. The coalition's first action was a call for nationally coordinated local actions on December 10, Human Rights Day. More than 130 events took place that day all over the United States, generating substantial local and regional press coverage for the growing antiwar movement. At the University of Michigan demonstrators created a symbolic graveyard at the main walkway through campus. In Providence, Rhode Island, a hundred people staged a die-in at the downtown federal

Cobblestones decorated with symbols of peace grace the streets of New York City in preparation for the February 15 antiwar rally (photo, Nathan Blaney).

building. Demonstrations took place at federal buildings in Oakland and Sacramento. At the U.S. mission to the United Nations in New York, more than one hundred protesters were arrested—including Daniel Ellsberg, Ben Cohen, and Reverend Herbert Daughtry of the House of the Lord Church in Brooklyn. None of the protests were huge, but this first wave of coordinated local action represented an important beginning for the new antiwar coalition. The December 10 actions were a significant success, according to Cagan, and "spoke to the real breadth of opposition to what the Bush administration was doing."[5]

As United for Peace and Justice discussed options for a national protest demonstration, it had to contend with ANSWER, which had already obtained permits and issued a call for a rally in Washington on January 18, 2003, the weekend of the Martin Luther King, Jr. national holiday. Rather than attempt to compete with the ANSWER rally in Washington, United for Peace and Justice called for demonstrations in New York on February 15 and in San Francisco on the sixteenth. The February 15 date was selected to coincide with global antiwar protests proposed by activists at the November 2002 European Social Forum in Florence, Italy.[6] The call for a mass demonstration in New York in the middle of winter was risky. No one knew if the protest would be successful. Organizing for the rally did not even begin until the second week in

January. The mobilizing effort combined traditional methods of activist recruitment with the innovative potential of the Internet. More than a million leaflets were distributed in New York and in nearby states, and announcements were sent via the Internet, as visits to the United for Peace and Justice website soon reached two million a day. The United for Peace and Justice website became a central bulletin board for the antiwar movement, offering action plans, contact information, news updates, and organizing tips.

The outreach effort for February 15 benefited from decades of experience among veterans like Cagan, and drew energy from a new, younger activist movement that had emerged in response to globalization challenges and September 11.[7] The gathering momentum of the planned rallies around the world added excitement and energy to the organizing effort in the U.S. In the end the public moment turned out to be exactly right, as popular alarm over the Bush administration's war policies peaked in the United States and throughout the world, producing the historic mass demonstrations of February 15, 2003.

United for Peace and Justice continued to organize protest actions until and after the war began. One of the biggest actions came in New York on March 22. The demonstration had been announced a couple of weeks before but came just as the war was beginning. The crowd that day rivaled the turnout on February 15. An estimated three hundred thousand people streamed onto Broadway north of 34th Street and marched down to Washington Square Park. At one point the crowd completely filled Broadway for the entire length of the march. It was an overwhelming turnout that stunned even the organizers. Cagan recalled thinking, "Where are all these people coming from? We're not that good." For many New Yorkers, like herself, the demonstration was a reaction to 9/11, and the Bush administration's manipulation of the city's suffering. "For those of us who lived through 9/11, there was a sense that we never wanted to see that kind of horror visited on other people, whether by a small group of terrorists or by the state terrorism of a military invasion."[8]

Win Without War

The October 25, 2002 meeting in Washington that resulted in the formation of United for Peace and Justice also spurred the creation of the Win Without War coalition. Several of us who attended the larger meeting were impatient with the tedious process and lack of focus during the all-day session. We decided to meet for dinner that evening at a

Protesters fill the streets of New York for the February 15 peace rally (photo, Devin Asch).

nearby Chinese restaurant. I had prepared a concept paper outlining the idea of creating a more structured and focused committee of mainstream national organizations with a streamlined decision-making process. The others around the table—Alistair Millar of the Fourth Freedom Forum, Susan Shaer of WAND, Eli Pariser of MoveOn, Duane Peterson of True Majority, Melissa Daar of Working Assets—had been thinking similarly, and we agreed to begin working together to create such a committee. Our goal was to build a coalition that could attract major constituency organizations, not just traditional peace groups. We wanted a quick and efficient decision-making process. We believed that the political message of the activist movement should emphasize containing and disarming Saddam Hussein without war. We also felt the need for an effective public relations and communications campaign to reach mainstream audiences. Other groups that agreed to come together on the basis of these understandings included the National Council of Churches, Sojourners, the United Methodist Church, Physicians for Social Responsibility, the Sierra Club, the National Organization for Women, and the National Association for the Advancement of Colored People. Forty organizations eventually joined the new national coalition, which was officially launched at a press conference in Washington on December 11.

The development of the new coalition and of the antiwar movement benefited enormously from a planning and strategy retreat the weekend of November 15–17, 2002 at Blue Mountain Retreat Center in the Adirondack mountains of upstate New York. The session was hosted by Harriet Barlow, director of the center, who played an indispensable role in organizing financial support for the emerging movement. It was during a creative brainstorming session at Blue Mountain that the name "Win Without War" was selected. Participants agreed on a proactive and positive political message: the United States and the United Nations can disarm Iraq and enhance security through vigorous weapons inspections and continued containment. Many acknowledged the need for a sophisticated and large-scale public relations effort to communicate a patriotic antiwar message. Participants also recognized the need for close cooperation between Win Without War and United for Peace and Justice. The two coalitions would have different emphases—grassroots demonstrations for United for Peace and Justice, media communications for Win Without War—but they would strive to share information and coordinate their efforts.

In practice the coordination between United for Peace and Justice and Win Without War was limited. Within United for Peace and Justice there were concerns about the development of Win Without War. Bill Fletcher noted that some activists were "perplexed" by the creation of a parallel coalition.[9] At the first Win Without War meeting in December, the need for the new group was questioned by Medea Benjamin, director of Global Exchange and a founder of United for Peace and Justice. Bob Edgar of the National Council of Churches explained that the coalition would have a speedier and more efficient decision-making process, a greater emphasis on public relations, and a narrower political agenda focused on stopping the war. Some activist leaders, such as Peace Action director Kevin Martin, saw value in having two coalitions so that the movement could reach out both to the left and the center.[10] The two coalitions maintained friendly relations, and there was some overlap in membership, with the American Friends Service Committee, Peace Action, Global Exchange, and other groups participating in both coalitions. A de facto division of labor developed, with United for Peace and Justice focusing on the mobilization of grassroots protest, while Win Without War emphasized Internet organizing and media communications.

One of the first decisions of the new Win Without War coalition was to create an effective leadership structure. We chose two national co-chairs, Susan Shaer and Bob Edgar. We hired Lynn Erskine as campaign coordinator and began the search for a national director/spokesperson. By this time public alarm about war was spreading rapidly, and money to support our cause was pouring in. We were in the rare and fortunate position of having the resources to hire a professional. One of the first persons we approached was former member of Congress Tom Andrews. Andrews had represented the first district of Maine in the House of Representatives for six years and served as a member of the powerful House Armed Services Committee. He was known and respected as one of the most effective progressive leaders in Congress, with a stellar voting record on issues of peace and arms control. Prior to being elected to Congress Andrews had been a community organizer and progressive leader in Maine for a variety of causes. Following his congressional service, Andrews created his own media advocacy firm, New Economy Communications, and worked on a range of human rights campaigns. As the threat of war loomed, Andrews served as an adviser for the antiwar media project created by Fenton Communications, where he shared office space. Andrews was thoroughly familiar with the issues and arguments against war, and he shared our shock and dismay at the prospect of the United States invading Iraq. He agreed to become national director and served as chief strategist and spokesperson for the coalition. His extensive political experience and creative organizing and speaking abilities were an enormous asset for the movement. He appeared on numerous national talk show programs and was respected by the national media as an articulate and reasoned opponent of war. More than any single person, Andrews became the national media voice of the antiwar movement.

Virtual organizing became the métier of the Win Without War coalition, as it mobilized the vast membership networks of its Internet-based groups and constituency organizations for coordinated lobbying and action campaigns. Its most ambitious effort was the "virtual march on Washington" on February 26, 2003. Citizens all over the United States that day phoned, faxed, or e-mailed their elected representatives to oppose the march to war. Andrews conceived the plan as a way of harnessing the grassroots organizing power of MoveOn, True Majority, and other coalition member groups to apply focused political pressure on Congress. The point was not to back any specific congressional legislation but to demonstrate the organized clout of the antiwar movement, in the hope that legislators would redirect pressure for military restraint onto the White House. Win Without War mounted a huge outreach effort, mobilizing the networks of churches, women's groups, campus committees, environmentalists, and a wide range of constituencies. All across Capitol Hill on February 26, the phones and fax machines were jammed. Members of Congress reported receiving hundreds and even thousands of messages by early afternoon that day. It was impossible to

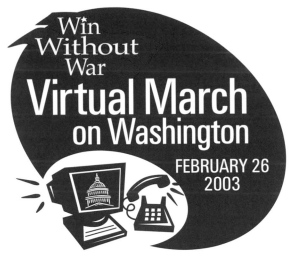

The virtual march on Washington sponsored by the Win Without War coalition.

www.MoveOn.org/WinWithoutWar

calculate the exact number of messages, but Andrews estimated that more than one million calls, faxes, and e-mail messages were sent. It was one of the largest one-day lobbying efforts in U.S. political history. Coming just eleven days after the massive street demonstrations of February 15, the virtual march was further evidence of the vast scale of the movement against war.

In the final weeks before the invasion, the Win Without War coalition maintained a frenetic pace of activity in a desperate attempt to prevent an increasingly certain military attack. Relying primarily on the rapidly expanding membership networks of MoveOn and True Majority, Win Without War launched an international petition to the UN Security Council urging rejection of a U.S. and British draft resolution authorizing war. The response was overwhelming, the greatest of any MoveOn petition, and undoubtedly one of the most successful mass petitions in history. Within days, more than one million people signed the Security Council petition. It was delivered to UN representatives in New York at a Win Without War/MoveOn press conference on March 10. At the same time the coalition issued an international call for antiwar vigils the following weekend, March 15–16. Once again the response was overwhelming, as thousands of groups all over the world announced plans to hold candlelight and prayer vigils in their communities. More than six thousand vigils took place in more than one hundred countries that weekend. Once again the world said no to war, this time in a prayerful plea at the last hour before the onset of military hostilities. It was the most diverse and widespread international wave of local peace action ever organized,

Thousands gather on the Washington Mall for a candlelight vigil, March 2003 (AP photo, Evan Vucci).

another powerful indication of the unprecedented scale of the global movement against war.

E-Activism

Much of the success of Win Without War and the antiwar movement in general can be ascribed to the powerful impact of Internet organizing, and the specific role of MoveOn and True Majority. The Internet emerged as a tool of mass political mobilization in the campaign against the impeachment of President Bill Clinton in 1998 and in the broader global justice movement that emerged in 1999. It was not until the Iraq antiwar movement, however, that the full range of possibilities for utilizing the Internet for social change organizing became evident. The global justice movement used the Internet effectively as a means of communication, coordination, and education among decentralized networks of organizers around the world. To these functions antiwar activists added new dimensions of Internet mobilization: the development of organized "membership" networks, the creation of "meeting tools" to facilitate coordinated local action, and online fundraising. The result was an unprecedented capacity to raise consciousness and mobilize political action.

MoveOn was the pioneer and leading force in this Internet revolution. It was the largest group within Win Without War and served as the backbone of the movement's most extensive organizing and communication efforts. In August 2002, as antiwar actions were beginning to emerge, MoveOn organized hundreds of local meetings in which constituents urged their members of Congress to oppose war. Prior to the congressional vote in October, MoveOn circulated an antiwar petition to Congress signed by hundreds of thousands of people. After the vote, in a tribute to the twenty-three senators who stood against the resolution,

MoveOn launched a campaign to "reward the heroes." It appealed for online contributions to antiwar members of Congress who faced difficult reelection campaigns, most importantly Minnesota senator Paul Wellstone. The response was overwhelming, and set a record for online fundraising. In a matter of days, MoveOn raised more than $2 million, including $700,000 for the Wellstone campaign. Tragically, the senator died in a plane crash a few days later. When the news of Wellstone's death arrived during the United for Peace and Justice founding meeting in Washington on October 25, there was stunned shock. Several people wept openly, and the meeting was suspended for a time. The loss of Wellstone was a crushing blow to many antiwar activists, who took encouragement from his principled vote against war, and hoped that his reelection could send a message to other Democrats that standing up for peace is good politics.

MoveOn played a central role in building support for major antiwar actions, including the February 15 rallies, the virtual march on Washington, the petition to the UN Security Council, and the worldwide antiwar vigils in March 2003. All of this action flowed from an organization with a tiny staff of seven people working from their homes—an organization with a powerful computer and sophisticated software system, but no office and none of the usual accoutrements of traditional membership groups.[11] In the six months leading up to the outbreak of war in March 2003, MoveOn's online network, U.S. and international, jumped from approximately seven hundred thousand to nearly two million. Win Without War contributed to this membership growth by steering contacts to the organization and using MoveOn as a central repository for new names.

Other electronically based networks also experienced extraordinary growth and activity during the antiwar movement. True Majority was founded by Ben Cohen in June 2002 as a progressive, Internet-based activist network. It grew rapidly as the antiwar movement emerged, reaching one hundred thousand members by the end of 2002 and 350,000 a year later.[12] Working in close partnership with Business Leaders for Sensible Priorities, True Majority specialized in producing bold, visually appealing newspaper ads and Internet messages that helped to attract new supporters. True Majority also developed a partnership with the National Council of Churches, helping to reach and mobilize religious leaders and faith-based activists throughout the country. Working Assets represented a different kind of electronic activist network. Founded in 1985 as a progressive telecommunications company offering long-distance, wireless, and credit card services, Working Assets developed a

THEY'RE SELLING WAR.

WE'RE NOT BUYING.

The President's men have compared their war on Iraq to a new product. They've timed it "from a marketing point of view." They're supporting it with "a multimillion-dollar PR blitz." But their product is a deadly distraction bristling with nasty side effects. Speaking as seasoned business people, we want to see warnings on the label:

WARNING
WAR WILL WRECK ECONOMY

America is teetering on the brink of renewed recession. People are hurting. People are scared. For the first time in a decade median household income is down; poverty rates and unemployment are up; the gap between rich and poor is growing; the huge surpluses of the last years have vanished into huge deficits; state, city and school budgets across the country are in shock; the stock market has plummeted to 5-year lows. Is anybody up there paying attention? Do they think their war will fix things? How can blowing up buildings and killing people be good for business, unless it's the body-bag business? How can the oil price spikes that inevitably follow Mideast conflict wreak anything but havoc? War will just burn up the money that *could* fix things. White House estimate of the war's cost: up to $200 billion. Imagine what we could do with $200 billion! We could pay 200,000 new teachers, police, and firefighters salaries for 10 years...*and* build 10,000 new schools!

WARNING
WAR WILL BREED TERRORISM

Arab friends warn us: An invasion of Iraq will open "the gates of hell." People may hate tyrants, but they hate foreign invaders more. "I will throw stones at them," said a Baghdad woman; "Maybe I will throw knives," said another. The brutal images of war can be sanitized for U.S. viewers; they won't be sanitized for the rest of the world. Bombings, slaughter, "collateral damage" will make recruitment posters for a new generation of terrorists. The final winner of war with Iraq will be Osama bin Laden.

WARNING
WAR WILL DISCREDIT AMERICA
IN THE WORLD'S EYES

Virtually no other nation in the world really wants this war. Most of them dread it. We can buy their silence, cajole their leaders,

ram war down their throats, but the world's eyes are open: Far from showing the "decent respect for the opinions of mankind" our Declaration of Independence requires, the President is showing his contempt.

WARNING
WAR WILL TAKE A TERRIBLE
TOLL IN HUMAN LIFE

The White House is after one man, but to get him they'll have to kill tens or hundreds of thousands more. Most of the victims will be innocent Iraqis. Many will be children. In each major war since World War I, the ratio of non-combatant deaths to combatant deaths has grown worse. As to U.S. casualties? No one dares say, but we know the Generals' fears: "It's not going to be an easy battle"(Schwarzkopf) "...high casualties on both sides"(Hoar) "very expensive ...and could as well be bloody"(Scowcroft) "...all the generals see it the same way." (Zinni)

War is hell. Those who've been to war know that. Only fools rush into hell. We urge the President: Slow down. Put off the new product launch. Give the U.N. a chance. Get to work on the neglected tasks here at home.

Polls show majority support for the course proposed here. To make sure your voice is heard in Washington, go to TrueMajority.com. And to help spread this message, please make a tax-deductible contribution to Business Leaders for Sensible Priorities.

BUSINESS LEADERS FOR SENSIBLE PRIORITIES
TrueMajority Campaign
P.O. Box 1976 Old Chelsea Station
New York, NY 10113

Ben Cohen, President

Dear Ben,
I will not stand by and allow an unprovoked invasion in my name. Please use my enclosed tax-deductible contribution of $_____ to make sure the American people hear the case against war with Iraq.

Name

Address

City   State   Zip

Phone   e-mail

To sign up for our on-line campaign, visit us at **truemajority.com** customer/subscriber base of several hundred thousand households. It donated a portion of its revenues to support organizations working for peace, human rights, equality, education, and the environment. Over the years it contributed $35 million for these causes. Working Assets also mobilized its customers to engage in progressive action through notices that were included with monthly subscriber bills. As the antiwar movement developed, Working Assets naturally became involved and developed web-based organizing tools. During the Iraq debate, Working Assets generated more than 430,000 online actions, letters, and calls in opposition to Bush administration policy. The organization also raised over $465,000 for antiwar efforts in the U.S. and humanitarian relief/democracy building activities in Iraq.[13]

When Internet organizing began, some skeptics questioned the value of a tool that kept activists glued to their computer screens. The very ease with which one could click and send off a message, sometimes to hundreds of recipients, seemed to cheapen the value of the effort. Lobbyists reported that the impact of an e-mail message as a form of political communication paled in comparison with that of other messages, such as a letter, phone call, or personal visit. MoveOn and the other Internet-based activist groups recognized these limitations early on and devised methods of mobilization that significantly broadened the impact of e-mail activism. One significant innovation was the use of the Internet to organize coordinated local meetings. Activists were encouraged to get up from their computer screens and go out to meetings where they could connect with other activists in their communities. MoveOn developed a meeting tool that Pariser termed "action in a box." Campaigns were user-friendly and were programmed so that respondents could be led easily through a series of prompts offering venues and functions for action. An e-mail message from MoveOn would contain the call to action, and by clicking the appropriate icons, the respondent could be connected to other activists and could volunteer for various tasks, ranging from attending a meeting and sending an e-mail to Congress, to more ambitious duties such as coordinating a meeting, speaking in public, and contacting the media. Working Assets developed a similar meeting tool, which gave subscribers options for participating in local activities. By segmenting lists according to location and interest, Internet organizers could use their membership bases to sponsor highly particularized forms of action. The success of the meetings at local congressional offices organized by MoveOn in August 2002 confirmed the effectiveness of the Internet as a tool for political lobbying.

Equally important in translating Internet communications into political power was the development and use of online fundraising. Just as online marketing has become increasingly significant in the commercial economy, Internet-based fundraising has rapidly become a vital source of income for social movements, nonprofit groups, and political campaigns. MoveOn's first foray into antiwar fundraising, its "reward the heroes" campaign of October 2002, paved the way for a series of subsequent appeals for donations to finance paid advertising and public relations efforts. In the months preceding the war MoveOn raised more than $1 million for newspaper and television ads and associated public relations activities, thus turning its vast Internet network into a crucial source of financial support for the antiwar movement. After the invasion, MoveOn became a fundraising powerhouse, fueling the initial presidential drive of Howard Dean and generating millions of dollars for advertising and public relations efforts to expose the Bush administration's deceit in misleading the country into war.

Social movement theory emphasizes the importance of resource mobilization as a means of exerting political influence. Movements are linked to social change organizations, which depend upon formal dues-paying membership networks. These structures provide a sustained and predictable base of income and activism. Traditional membership networks also offer opportunities for participatory decision making, with individual members or chapters playing a role in determining organizational priorities and selecting leaders. The Internet-based networks of MoveOn and True Majority are less formal and more loosely structured. There are no annual dues or membership requirements, no chapters or affiliates, indeed no fixed organizational structure at all. The "members" of MoveOn participate only to the extent that they feel motivated to respond to particular e-mail action alerts. It is an approach, said writer Andrew Boyd, that "embraces the permission-based culture of the Internet, and consumer culture itself."[14] Pariser described this as a "postmodern organizing model."[15]

This new form of organizing raises important questions about traditional models of social change. The classic theory, followed by Gandhi, King, and other great nonviolent leaders, is that political impact depends on organizational strength. In his extensive organizing experience Saul Alinsky found an indispensable connection between building organizations and achieving political results. Alinsky wrote in *Rules for Radicals*: "power and organization are one and the same thing."[16] In *Strategic Nonviolent Conflict*, scholars Peter Ackerman and Christopher Kruegler emphasized the importance of "efficient, fighting organizations" as crucial elements of successful social action.[17] MoveOn and other Internet-based groups only partly follow this model. They provide networks for fundraising and coordinated action, but do not create long-term institutional structures. The memberships of these groups consist of atomized individuals rather than networks of organized affiliates. There are no formalized mechanisms for grassroots decision making or structured feedback on group policies. In June 2003 MoveOn asked members to interview each other by phone to find out what issues and values were considered most important. Nearly twenty thousand members participated, producing ten thousand pages of feedback. This type of informal polling can be helpful in determining overall priorities, but decisions on actual program are decided by the small MoveOn staff and then communicated to the network. Over time this approach may have a disempowering effect on the "members" and lead to diminishing participation. If systems for sustaining involvement and interest are not developed, the huge networks generated during the antiwar movement may prove ephemeral. This does not mean necessarily that these groups should attempt to create formal institutions. The costs of building and maintaining an affiliate network and formal membership structure can be huge, and may drain resources from other priorities. Institutional sclerosis can sometimes drag down a large organization. A better model might be to preserve the spontaneity and flexibility of the Internet-based groups, while finding ways of using their vast membership and fundraising potential to strengthen existing membership organizations.

During the antiwar movement, organizations with more traditional membership bases also developed e-mail networks and increased their fundraising potential. The religiously based organization, Sojourners, saw its newly-created Sojo list expand from twenty thousand in the summer of 2002 to more than seventy thousand in March 2003. Peace Action, the Council for a Livable World, and other organizations also developed e-mail listservs and experienced tremendous growth in electronic participation. All of these groups used the Internet as a mechanism for political communication and fundraising. The use of electronic organizing and the overall growth of antiwar activism led to significant membership increases in most of the established peace organizations. WAND, Peace Action, and Physicians for Social Responsibility all reported 20 percent increases in membership during the antiwar campaign.[18] The movement against war in Iraq thus became an opportunity for traditional peace groups to grow organizationally and financially.

Notes

1. Bill Fletcher, interview by author, 16 December 2003.

2. Chris Hedges, "A Long-time Antiwar Activist, Escalating the Peace," *New York Times*, 4 February 2003, B2.

3. Leslie Cagan, interview by author, 26 August 2003.

4. Van Gosse, "February 15, 2003 in New York: A Preliminary Assessment," 17 February 2003, <http://www.yachana.org/haw/feb15van.html> (accessed 21 November 2003).

5. Cagan, interview.

6. Mark LeVine, "The Peace Movement Plans for the Future," *Middle East Report* (July 2003), <http://www.merip.org/mero/interventions/levine_interv.html> (accessed 24 November 2003).

7. Gosse, "February 15, 2003 in New York."

8. Cagan, interview.

9. Fletcher, interview.

10. Kevin Martin, interview by author, 4 December 2003.

11. For a portrait of MoveOn, see Michelle Goldberg, "MoveOn Moves Up," *Salon* (1 December 2003), <http://archive.salon.com/news/feature/2003/12/01/moveon/print.html> (accessed 15 December 2003).

12. Gary Ferdman, interview by author, 23 December 2003.

13. Melissa Daar, e-mail message to author, 23 December 2003.

14. Andrew Boyd, "The Web Rewires the Movement," *The Nation* 277, no. 4 (4–11 August 2003): 14.

15. Quoted in Boyd, "The Web Rewires the Movement."

16. Saul Alinsky, *Rules for Radicals: A Practical Primer for Realistic Radicals* (New York: Vintage Books, 1971), 113.

17. Peter Ackerman and Christopher Kruegler, *Strategic Nonviolent Conflict: The Dynamics of People Power in the 20th Century* (Westport, Conn.: Praeger, 1994), 26.

18. Based on personal conversations by author with the directors of the three organizations—Susan Shaer, Kevin Martin, and Bob Musil—September 2003.

Chapter Three

The World Speaks

Of the many extraordinary features of the antiwar movement, none was more remarkable than its international dimension. Organized opposition to U.S. policy emerged in every part of the world and was expressed in countless statements, petitions, and demonstrations. The protests of February 15, 2003 were literally a global phenomenon, with reports of antiwar action that weekend in more than six hundred cities. In nearly every country, opinion polls showed solid and sometimes overwhelming majorities against U.S.-led military action in Iraq. In some countries people considered George W. Bush more of a threat to international security than Saddam Hussein.[1] In the United States the global movement was a source of inspiration for those of us who spoke out. We gained confidence and strength in knowing that we were standing with the vast majority of the world's people. For a few incredible months the human family joined together as never before, united in a fervent plea for peace.

The plan for coordinated international actions on February 15 was conceived at the European Social Forum in Florence, Italy, in November 2002. The initial call urged groups and individuals in Europe and beyond to organize massive opposition to the U.S. attack through antiwar demonstrations in the capital of every nation on February 15. Further preparations took place a month later in Copenhagen, with representatives of United for Peace and Justice also in attendance. The final plans were laid at the World Social Forum, which took place January 23 through 27 in Porte Allegre, Brazil. Thousands of global justice activists participated in the Forum and helped to spread the call throughout the world. In dozens of countries national coalitions were created, encompassing a wide range of movements and organizations. The U.K. had the Stop the War Coalition, Italy *Fermiamo la Guerra all'Iraq,* Germany *Netzwerk Friedenskooperative,* Spain *No al la Guerra.* All the national coalitions set up websites that were linked to each other. Many adopted the same slogan and graphic symbol, a missile crossed out with the words "stop the war."[2]

The February 15 demonstration in London was the largest in the history of that city, and perhaps of any other. It was a typically gray February day, but the rain held off and it was not bitterly cold. The crowd embarked from two separate assembly sites, pouring into and filling much of Hyde Park. More than one million people overflowed the city's center.[3] One of the speakers that day was Reverend Jesse Jackson, Sr., who traveled to London as the guest of Mayor Ken Livingstone. Jackson gamely joined the march despite having a cast on his foot from recent surgery. When Jackson was introduced on stage, according to long-time aide Steve Cobble, "the response from the crowd was

Over one million antiwar protestors march through London on February 15 (AP photo, Andrew Parsons).

electrifying. A roar started up, similar to the 'wave' at a football game, rolling from front to back, a huge greeting of welcome. The goose bumps stood up on my arms."[4] Jackson's speech was well received, one of the most remarkable in his long career of oratory.

The London march was accompanied by hundreds of peace demonstrations that day in every part of the world. Tens of thousands marched in Glasgow, Dublin, and Belfast. Rivaling the demonstration in London was a massive protest of perhaps one million people in Rome. The historic heart of the city, between the Coliseum and Piazza San Giovanni, was packed for hours by a slow-moving procession of protesters. Half a million people assembled in Madrid, while the crowd in Barcelona was estimated at one million. Smaller protests occurred in Valencia, Seville, Los Palmas, and Cadiz. Half a million marched in Berlin, and crowds of one hundred thousand or more gathered in Brussels, Paris, and Athens, with smaller protests in more than one hundred other European cities. More than one hundred thousand demonstrated in Montreal, Toronto, Vancouver, and other Canadian cities. Tens of

Antiwar demonstrators in Antarctica add their voices to the global protest against the war (photo, Rick Sterling).

thousands turned out in Mexico City, Rio de Janeiro, Montevideo, and Buenos Aires. Several hundred thousand gathered in Sydney and Melbourne. In New Zealand, protests took place in Auckland, Wellington, and more than a dozen other cities. Thousands marched in Tokyo, Seoul, Bangkok, Manila, Kuala Lumpur, Jakarta (the week before), Lahore, New Delhi, Calcutta, and other Asian cities. Approximately twenty thousand people marched in Johannesburg, Cape Town, and Durban. In Damascus some two hundred thousand demonstrated at the People's Assembly. Tens of thousands rallied in Beirut and Amman. Several thousand people, Jews and Palestinians together, marched in Tel Aviv. A few hearty souls even demonstrated in Antarctica.

More important than the number and extent of these demonstrations was their political impact. Opposition to war was especially broad in those countries where the government supported the U.S.-led war effort. In Great Britain, Spain, and Italy, citizens said no while their political leaders were saying yes. In Spain and Italy opinion polls showed more than 80 percent of the public opposed to participating in the U.S.-led war. In Poland, although there was little organized protest, more than 70 percent opposed participation in the war.

In Germany antiwar sentiment played a decisive role in swaying the outcome of national elections. Social Democratic Chancellor Gerhard Schröder won a narrow come-from-behind victory in the September 2002 elections by emphasizing his opposition to war in Iraq. For months

Schröder had lagged behind in the polls because of widespread misgivings about his economic policies. As public alarm about the war spread, Schröder cobbled together a successful electoral strategy by consciously exploiting voters' antiwar sentiments and sharpening his criticism of U.S. policy. One international news report quipped, "Schröder beats Bush in German election."[5] The vote not only kept a strongly antiwar Schröder in office, but also elevated the Green Party to new heights, further strengthening the position of Foreign Minister and Green Party leader Joschka Fischer. The election results reinforced international opposition to war because of Germany's position on the UN Security Council, and it enhanced the influence of environmental and peace forces in German domestic politics.

Perhaps the most remarkable manifestation of antiwar sentiment occurred in Turkey, where a popularly elected parliament refused the Bush administration's request to use the country as a base and transit corridor for U.S. invasion forces. The *Washington Post* called Turkey's rejection "a stunning setback" to the Bush administration's war plans.[6] Ankara's decision went against a tradition of decades of close military cooperation between Turkey and the United States. Turkish leaders also turned aside a huge package of financial inducements offered by Washington, including $6 billion in direct grants and up to $20 billion in loan guarantees.[7] The Turkish decision had direct military impact. The United States had planned to deploy more than sixty thousand troops in Turkey, including a strike force from the Fourth Infantry Division. The battle plan against Iraq called for a two-pronged attack from both north and south. U.S. officials were so confident of Turkish cooperation that more than thirty military transport ships were on their way or already deployed off Turkey's Mediterranean coast as the decision was being made. Several hundred U.S. support troops were in Turkey renovating bases and ports in preparation for the invasion force. Parliament's last-minute rejection forced Pentagon planners to redeploy the Fourth Division and other troops to the south, creating a more complicated and difficult invasion scenario.

The rejection of war in Turkey came from a democratic, moderate Islamist government—precisely the kind of regime U.S. officials claim to want for Iraq and other Middle East countries. The problem for U.S. officials was that an expression of democratic sentiment meant rejection of American policy. Turkey's Justice and Development Party had won the November 2002 elections in part by appealing to popular opposition to U.S. war plans. A March 2003 poll by the Pew Research Center for the People and the Press measured antiwar opposition in Turkey at 86 per-

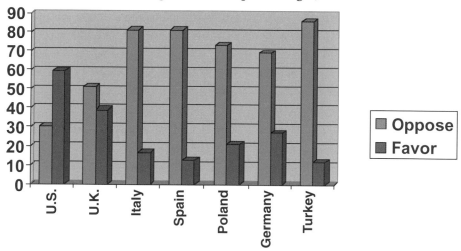

International Antiwar Opinion:
Oppose or Favor Military Action[8]

(Figures are in percentages)

Legend: ■ Oppose ■ Favor

cent. Some three hundred thousand people demonstrated in Ankara as members of parliament gathered to vote on March 1. The legislators were under enormous pressure, pulled by a powerful ally to provide military cooperation, pushed by an energized domestic constituency to represent the overwhelming popular rejection of war. It was a critically important moment for the young Justice and Development Party, which was trying to create a more democratic, yet Islamist, tradition in Turkish politics. When the parliamentary votes were tallied, the resolution to approve the U.S. request fell three votes short of the needed majority. Officials in Washington immediately demanded a revote, but Turkish leaders refused, fearing that an attempt to overturn the vote would bring down the government. The Turkish people and their elected representatives had spoken. The answer was no.

There were countless other global antiwar expressions. In Australia the Senate voted to censure Prime Minister John Howard for agreeing to deploy troops to Iraq without parliamentary approval. It was the first no-confidence vote in the chamber's 102-year history. Australian opinion polls showed 76 percent of the public against participation in a war without UN backing.[9] In South Korea Roh Moo Hyun won the presidency in December 2002 in part by riding a tide of anti-American sentiment. In his political campaign Roh vowed to continue the conciliatory "sunshine" policy toward North Korea of his predecessor, Kim Dai Jung, rather than the confrontational approach favored by the Bush administration. Roh's electoral victory was the third among long-term American allies based upon popular rejection of U.S. foreign policy. In Pakistan, the elections of October 2002 showed a significant gain for pro-Taliban, anti-American religious parties. A group of six hard-line parties, campaigning on a platform that included sharp criticism of U.S. policy, won a higher than expected number of seats in Pakistan's national assembly and gained a majority in the North-West frontier near the Afghanistan border.[10] The election results were more anti-American than antiwar, but they were another sign of deepening political opposition to the United States around the world.

The significance of the pervasive international rejection of U.S. policy can scarcely be exaggerated. The antiwar movement had a major impact on global consciousness. It prevented Washington from winning UN support for military action in Iraq, and undermined international confidence in U.S. leadership. Former president Jimmy Carter wrote, "The heartfelt sympathy and friendship offered to America after the 9/11 attacks, even from formerly antagonistic regimes, has been largely dissipated; increasingly unilateral and domineering policies have brought international trust in our country to its lowest level in memory."[11] Washington's defeat at the UN Security Council undermined the legitimacy of American policy, and contributed to Turkey's rejection of U.S. basing rights, which disrupted military planning. When the invasion began no major government other than Britain agreed to participate. This added to the U.S. military burden. In the postwar occupation Washington's efforts to recruit a substantial international force were largely unsuccessful. As of December 2003, only 24,000 international troops were in Iraq, half of them from the United Kingdom, the rest consisting of modest contingents from Poland, Italy, Spain, Ukraine, Bulgaria, and an array of smaller countries. Nor was Washington successful in gaining substantial financial support for Iraq's reconstruction. Having pushed ahead with the invasion against the advice of virtually the entire world, Washington was left on its own to attempt to deal with the violent and chaotic aftermath. The United States paid a high price for alienating international opinion and rejecting the global plea for peace.

Faith-based Activism

The religious community played a central role in the Iraq antiwar movement, as it has in many important movements for peace and social justice.[12] Faith-based activists were the core and largest component of the grassroots antiwar movement.[13] Nearly every mainline Christian denomination—including the U.S. Conference of Catholic Bishops and most Protestant churches—issued public statements opposing war. Many religious leaders and members of local congregations participated in antiwar activities. Church-based opposition to war was broader in the case of Iraq than in any previous conflict in modern U.S. history. Faith-based activists were major players in the United for Peace and Justice and Win Without War coalitions. Bob Edgar and Jim Wallis were leaders in Win Without War and played important roles in mobilizing the religious community. Wallis and Edgar joined with John Chane, Episcopal Bishop of Washington, to organize a gathering of more than 3,500 religious leaders and other concerned citizens at the Washington National Cathedral on Martin Luther King, Jr. Day, January 21. That evening they led a dramatic candlelight procession from the cathedral to the White House. In early March Edgar spoke at an interfaith service at Grace Cathedral in San Francisco, cosponsored by Working Assets, where more than two thousand worshippers overflowed the sanctuary. Traditional religious peace groups—including the Catholic pacifist organization Pax Christi and groups within the Friends, Mennonite, and Brethren communities—played a leadership role in raising awareness and organizing expressions of antiwar concern.

The Jewish community showed less broadly-based opposition to war. Even reform constituencies such as the Union of American Hebrew Congregations remained silent in the face of the buildup to war, while more conservative and orthodox communities supported the administration's policies. This prowar stance reflected a right-wing, pro-Likud political tendency among some influential American Jewish leaders, in keeping with the position of the Sharon government in Israel. Saddam Hussein's virulent hostility toward the state of Israel and his government's support of anti-Israeli terrorist groups deeply troubled many. Nonetheless, some progressive Jewish groups actively supported the antiwar cause, including Jews for Peace in Palestine and Israel, the Tikkun Community, founded by Rabbi Michael Lerner, and the Shalom Center in Philadelphia, led by Rabbi Arthur Waskow. These were minority voices in the organized Jewish community, however. The lack of a substantial Jewish presence in the Iraq antiwar movement contrasted sharply with earlier antiwar movements, in which Jewish activists, intellectuals, and artists played important leadership roles. The lack of this creative force within the antiwar movement limited its overall effectiveness.

Just as the overall antiwar movement became internationalized to an unprecedented extent, so did its religious component. Never before

A giant rainbow flag with peace written in different languages is carried past the Coliseum during an antiwar demonstration in Rome, Italy, February 15, 2003 (AP photo, Fabio Sardella).

did so many religious leaders and organizations from around the world speak so forcefully against war. The most prominent voice was that of Pope John Paul II, who pleaded with world leaders to pursue diplomatic rather than military solutions. "War is always a defeat for humanity," the pope told assembled diplomats during his New Year address in January 2003. "War cannot be decided upon," he declared, "except as the very last option."[14] As the war began in March he urged people to continue standing against war. "It is ever more urgent to proclaim that only peace is the road to follow to construct a more just and united society."[15]

Senior Vatican officials were even more outspoken than the pope. Archbishop Renato Martino, head of the Pontifical Council for Justice and Peace, condemned unilateral or preventive military action as a "war of aggression."[16] Even Cardinal Joseph Ratzinger, the conservative Prefect of the Congregation for the Doctrine of the Faith, declared in September 2002: "The concept of 'preventive war' does not appear in the Catechism of the Catholic Church."[17] The Vatican had been opposed to the first Gulf War, but the opposition this time was much sharper, "almost apoplectic" in the words of one official. Church leaders saw Iraq as the test case for an ethically untenable preemptive war doctrine that undermined Catholic just war teaching and violated fifty years of international law. During the

Gulf War there was prudential concern. This time there was principled opposition.[18] National conferences of Catholic bishops in North America, Europe, Asia, and Africa joined the Vatican in issuing statements against war. The Vatican and several national Catholic conferences sent delegations to political leaders urging greater efforts for peace. The deliberative bodies of many other religious communities around the world joined in this faith-based outcry against war.

To help harness this international voice for peace, the U.S. National Council of Churches organized a series of religious delegation meetings with world leaders. In early February Bob Edgar led a delegation that met with senior religious leaders in Germany and then joined with these leaders in a one-hour session with German Chancellor Gerhard Schröder. The following week a National Council of Churches delegation visited Paris to confer with colleagues in the European Council of Churches and meet with aides to French President Jacques Chirac. The following weeks included similar visits to London for a fifty-minute meeting with Prime Minister Tony Blair, to Rome for meetings with Italian and Vatican officials, and to Moscow for sessions with Orthodox Church leaders and aides to President Vladimir Putin.[19]

Jim Wallis led the religious delegation that met with Blair in London in mid-February. That session featured one of the most significant initiatives of the church-based antiwar movement, a six-point plan for preventing war. The plan called for the indictment of Saddam Hussein on war crimes charges, and urged a vigorous multinational effort to disarm and contain the Iraqi dictator. Sojourners published the six-point plan in full-page advertisements in all of the major London newspapers on the day of the debate over war in Parliament. The six-point plan was a last-minute attempt to dissuade Blair and Bush from invading Iraq. It was also an attempt to influence public opinion by addressing ethical concerns about the crimes of Saddam Hussein and his Baathist government. The plan reflected Wallis' conviction that the antiwar movement needed to answer the "what about Saddam?" question. Blair was particularly vocal in making the case for war on the basis of the human rights atrocities committed by the Iraqi leader. For both ethical and practical reasons, Wallis believed, the movement had to take a tough stance toward Saddam. It was not enough simply to point to U.S. and U.K. complicity in previously supporting Saddam. That was true but insufficient as a moral and political argument. It was also necessary to acknowledge and condemn Saddam's brutal regime. The call for Saddam's indictment by an international criminal court was a concrete way of undermining the Iraqi leader's legitimacy and paving the way for his removal from office. The indictment of Serbian leader Slobodan Milosevic by a UN tribunal in June 1999 had been followed by his political downfall in October 2000. The proponents of indicting Saddam hoped that a similar fate might befall the Iraqi dictator. Wallis and his colleagues in the church community were in effect agreeing with the need for regime change in Baghdad, while remaining true to their nonviolent witness. They argued that legal, multilateral, nonmilitary means were available for disarming Iraq and countering Saddam Hussein.

Middle East scholar Mark LeVine has argued that the movement should have done more to address public concerns about the Iraqi dictator.[20] This might have helped to attract greater Jewish involvement in the antiwar movement. It was also a way of acknowledging and addressing the widespread perception of Saddam as evil incarnate. Sojourners and the Tikkun community called for the dictator's indictment, while simultaneously opposing a U.S. invasion, but most other groups were silent on the issue. Nor was there much critique of the oppressive nature of many other regimes in the region. This might have provided a rejoinder to those in Washington who argued that overthrowing Saddam would be a way of "democratizing the Middle East." There are limits to a movement's ability to develop a sophisticated ideology, however, especially when faced with such a rapid timetable for military action. Activists focused on a simple "no to war" message as the broadest theme for building and unifying the movement, and for communicating with the press. Perhaps with more time and reflection, the movement might have been able to follow the lead of Wallis and others in crafting a more nuanced message, but the necessary discussion and analysis never took place.

While not overtly against Saddam Hussein, the movement clearly was not for him either. The movement thus succeeded where past movements had failed. As Rebecca Solnit phrased it, the movement was able "to refuse the dichotomies. We were able to oppose a war in Iraq without endorsing Saddam Hussein. We were able to oppose a war with compassion for the troops who fought it."[21] The Iraq movement thus avoided the pitfalls of earlier movements, which in their solidarity for the victims of U.S. attack sometimes seemed in sympathy with armed revolutionaries. There was little chance of this happening in Iraq. Saddam Hussein was such an odious figure that few could find any redeeming merit in him or his regime. It was easy to avoid the trap of seeming to support the Iraqi dictatorship. The movement thus remained true to its nonviolent principles, and to its underlying commitment to universal democracy and human rights as the essential foundations of a world without war.

Prime Minister Blair, it is two minutes before midnight.

On February 18, five U.S. church leaders met with Prime Minister Tony Blair to discuss alternatives to war on Iraq. The plan in the following letter was developed from that discussion and subsequent conversations in the United States.

Prime Minister Blair, the world needs you to find a "third way" between war and inaction. It is two minutes before midnight, and the world's people are desperate for an alternative to war.

Yes, we must disarm Saddam Hussein.

Yes, we must remove him from power.

But, we need a better solution than war to accomplish our goals. The people of Iraq have already suffered greatly, and we must not inflict even more suffering upon them.

As Americans, we have a special relationship with the British people. We need you to be a true friend of America in this critical hour. We need you to help our goverment not make a terrible mistake.

American church leaders are offering an eleventh-hour initiative that proposes an effective response to the threat of Saddam Hussein and his weapons of mass destruction, but avoids the terrible dangers and suffering of war.

Mr. Prime Minister, we appeal to you as a man of moral and religious convictions to persuade our President not to take our countries into a war that could have terrible, bitter, and divisive consequences. Let us instead:

"WE NEED YOU TO BE A TRUE FRIEND OF AMERICA IN THIS CRITICAL HOUR."

1 Indict Saddam Hussein for his crimes against humanity and send a clear signal that he has no future in Iraq, setting into motion the internal and external forces that could remove him from power and bring him to trial at the International Court in The Hague. History has shown, as with Slobodan Milosevic, that this can help bring down a criminal regime.

2 Pursue coercive disarmament with greatly intensified inspections backed by a U.N. mandated multi-national force.

3 Foster a democratic Iraq through a temporary post-Hussein U.N. administration, rather than a U.S. military occupation.

4 Organize an effort through the U.N. and nongovernmental relief agencies for the people of Iraq now, rather than only after a war.

5 Commit to implement the "roadmap" to peace in the Middle East, with a clear timetable toward a two-state solution that guarantees a Palestinian state and a secure Israel by 2005.

6 Re-invigorate and sustain international cooperation in the campaign against terrorism, rather than having it disrupted by a divisive war against Iraq that intelligence officials believe will likely lead to further attacks.

Such a morally rooted and pragmatic initiative could help achieve an historic breakthrough and set a precedent for decisive and effective international action instead of war.

We urge you to provide the principled leadership and real friendship that could resolve this international crisis without war.

We are grateful for the recent meeting we had with you. You have our hopes and prayers.

Sincerely,

Jim Wallis
Executive Director and Editor-in-Chief of Sojourners

John Bryson Chane
Episcopal Bishop of Washington, D.C.

Clifton Kirkpatrick
Stated Clerk of the Presbyterian Church USA

Melvin Talbert
Ecumenical Officer of the United Methodist Council of Bishops

Daniel Weiss
Immediate Past General Secretary of the American Baptist Churches in the USA

and millions of concerned Americans

Read the complete 6-Point Plan at www.sojo.net/action or call Sojourners at 011-202-328-8842 for more information.

Sponsored by Business Leaders for Sensible Priorities

Labor

Trade unions played a major role in the Iraq antiwar movement. This was a new development for both the labor and peace movements. During the cold war trade unions in the United States often supported U.S. military action abroad and rarely participated in antiwar campaigns. During the Vietnam era, the AFL-CIO endorsed the war, and some construction union members in New York famously attacked antiwar demonstrators. Throughout the cold war the AFL-CIO actively collaborated with the CIA in a global campaign against left wing labor unions. While a progressive internationalist tradition also existed within labor—reflected by the labor committee for peace in Vietnam, the participation of the machinists and food workers unions in the nuclear freeze campaign, and the labor solidarity committee for Central America—trade unions generally were not part of the peace movement. Following the September 11 terrorist attacks, most unions supported the so-called war on terror. The president of the International Association of Machinists, R. Thomas Buffenbarger, openly called for a military campaign of vengeance.

As the debate over war in Iraq heated up, however, trade unions became decidedly skeptical about the proposed military overthrow of Saddam Hussein. A growing number of local unions and central labor councils adopted resolutions against war and began to speak out for alternative means of containing the Iraqi leader. In New York and other cities progressive union activists formed labor antiwar committees. A substantial U.S. antiwar labor movement emerged. It was initiated by Bob Muehlenkamp, who had served as organizing director for the Teamsters Union and vice president of 1199, New York's Health Care Union, and Gene Bruskin, secretary-treasurer of the Food and Allied Service Trades division of the AFL-CIO. Muehlenkamp and Bruskin were aided by the leaders of union locals and regional councils in dozens of cities. Antiwar labor activists came together for a January 2003 meeting in Chicago at which Bill Fletcher and I spoke. The more than one hundred delegates in attendance agreed to form a new organization, U.S. Labor Against the War. An unofficial tabulation at the Chicago meeting counted forty-two local unions, thirteen district or regional bodies, five national unions, twelve central labor councils, and five state federations that had passed antiwar resolutions. Many other union bodies adopted antiwar resolutions in subsequent weeks. In total more than three hundred local unions and committees, forty-five central labor councils, and seven national unions came out against the war.[22] The level of antiwar activity among trade unions far exceeded comparable opposition to any previous U.S. military action.

The executive council of the AFL-CIO passed a resolution at their winter meeting on February 27, 2003, officially declaring labor's opposition to a preemptive war fought without UN support. "The threat posed by Saddam Hussein deserves multilateral resolve," the executive council statement asserted, "not unilateral action." The council declared: "The president has not fulfilled his responsibility to make a compelling and coherent explanation to the American people and the world about the need for military action against Iraq at this time." If war comes, the council stated, it should be "truly a last resort, supported by both our allies and nations united."[23] The statement was hardly a ringing indictment of war, but it was an extraordinary departure from the AFL-CIO's positions on previous conflicts, and was another sign of deepening opposition to White House policy.

Not in Their Name

In addition to United for Peace and Justice and Win Without War, many other organizations and coalitions emerged to oppose war in Iraq. In September 2002 a full-page ad appeared in the *New York Times* under the banner "Not In Our Name." Initiated by activists connected to the Revolutionary Communist Party,[24] the Not In Our Name movement began in March and April 2002 as a reaction to the Bush administration's militarized response to September 11. The coalition raised three broad demands: "stop the war on the people of the world; stop the disappearances and vicious attacks on Arab, Muslim and South Asian people in the U.S.; and stop the destruction of civil, legal and political rights, including the very right to dissent, here in the U.S."[25] The coalition sponsored antiwar demonstrations in dozens of U.S. cities on the weekend of October 6, 2002, the first nationwide protests against war in Iraq. Approximately twenty-five thousand people rallied in New York's Central Park, while thousands marched in San Francisco's commercial district, in downtown Los Angeles, and in Seattle.[26]

Many others spoke up to dissociate themselves from the policy of unilateral attack espoused by the White House. On the opposite end of the political spectrum, more than thirty distinguished scholars of international security affairs, including leading proponents of the "realist" school of political philosophy, published an ad in the *New York Times* declaring war with Iraq "not in America's national interest."[27] Among the signers was University of Chicago professor John Mearsheimer, who appeared on broadcast interview programs and wrote articles arguing that the Iraqi military threat was effectively contained, and that invading Iraq would not contribute to the defense of the United States. Scientists also spoke out. In January forty-one U.S. Nobel laureates in science and economics, including eighteen National Medal of Science winners, issued a statement opposing "a preventive war against Iraq without broad international support."[28]

Students and youth also organized against the war, although in the few months available for antiwar activity the scale of campus protest did not reach that of the Vietnam era. Teach-ins and educational events occurred on hundreds of campuses in October 2002, and again in March 2003. The March events were billed as the International Student Day of Strike and Action against War in Iraq, a "Books not Bombs" speakout. It was initiated in the U.S. by the National Youth and Student Peace Coalition, which included the Student Environmental Action Coalition, Students Against Sanctions and War in Iraq, and United Students Against Sweatshops. Student groups also participated in Canada, Mexico, the U.K., France, Spain, Italy, Greece, and Australia.[29] In the U.S. nearly five hundred high school and college campuses participated in the March actions, which included teach-ins, mass leafletings, rallies, marches, debates, antiwar forums, and strikes. At some schools students engaged in a "walkout" from classes.[30] At dozens of universities student councils or faculty senates adopted resolutions opposing war. A faculty statement against war that began circulating in the fall was signed by more than ten thousand college and university professors.

One of the most significant grassroots initiatives was Cities for Peace, a campaign conceived by Marcus Raskin, founder and senior fellow of the Institute for Policy Studies in Washington D.C. The campaign emerged as a coalition of local elected officials and citizen groups working to convince city councils to adopt resolutions against war. The resolutions were individual to each town, city, county, or elected body, but all made links to international and national issues and had common themes: 1) opposition to Bush's preemptive strike doctrine; 2) affirmation of working through the United Nations and using diplomacy rather than military force; 3) skepticism about an imminent threat from Iraq; 4) alarm at the costs of war to state and local budgets; and 5) concern about the loss of life that war would bring. In all, some 165 city councils, representing forty million American citizens, adopted official resolutions opposing war.[31] Most major cities, including New York, Los Angeles, and Chicago, approved resolutions, along with a host of smaller municipalities. In some localities, such as Madison, convincing the city council to approve such a resolution was easy and required little community mobilization. In other instances, such as New York City, the reluctance of some officials made the task more challenging, and required a considerable local lobbying effort to win approval.

Grass Roots

Antiwar activities took place in thousands of communities in the United States and throughout the world. In some small and conservative localities, antiwar action emerged for the first time in many years. In communities with a history of activism, the events that occurred were larger and more frequent than in the past. A full rendering of the vast outpouring of grassroots organizing that was part of the antiwar movement is far beyond the limits of this short volume. But perhaps a brief look at two communities can give a glimpse of the extent of local activism. I focus here on the conservative rural region of northern Indiana where I live, and the liberal metropolis of Seattle.

In the wake of the September 11 attacks, American flags appeared everywhere in northern Indiana, as they did throughout the country. In several church communities, however, a different kind of response emerged. Students and faculty at Goshen College, a small Mennonite college, began to circulate a statement calling for reconciliation and justice, rather than revenge and war. They sent the statement to dozens of congregations and religious communities in South Bend, Elkhart, and Goshen, asking for signatures and contributions so that it could be placed in local newspapers. The response was overwhelming. More than eight hundred people signed the ad, contributing $14,000 for its dissemination. This was a huge sum for so small a community and enabled the group to place full-page ads in all the local newspapers.

As the discussion of invading Iraq heated up in the fall of 2002, educational events occurred at several local colleges and universities. At the University of Notre Dame the Joan B. Kroc Institute for International Peace Studies sponsored a series of faculty panels examining the security consequences and ethical implications of war. Hundreds of students and faculty attended these events. Professor George A. Lopez led off a student-sponsored dormitory series by questioning whether a preemptive attack without international authorization could meet the just war criteria of Catholic social teaching. It was a concern he repeated in a widely read article for the influential Catholic journal *Commonweal,* and which he presented to the U.S. Conference of Catholic Bishops as they prepared their statement on the war.[32] Students also participated in the war debate by organizing a teach-in at Goshen College in October and a "books not bombs" speakout at Notre Dame in March.

The northern Indiana chapter of Women's Action for New Directions (WAND) sponsored a radio advertising campaign. The campaign was the brainchild of Julia King, a writer and commentator for the Great Lakes Radio Consortium. The ads questioned the wisdom of war and ended with a simple plea to "think about it." King and chapter president Karen Jacob raised money from WAND members to purchase ads on a pop music station. The station manager initially questioned the content of the ads but later agreed to air them. The ads and the controversy they stirred generated coverage in broadcast and print media.[33] WAND chapters in Detroit and Little Rock borrowed the idea and sponsored similar radio ad campaigns in their communities.

Protest demonstrations are a rare occurrence in northern Indiana, but they occurred frequently in the months preceding the outbreak of war. One of the first actions occurred in October, when President Bush came to South Bend to campaign for the local Republican candidate for Congress. When word of the president's visit was announced, antiwar groups and local trade unions announced plans to organize protests. The two groups coordinated their actions and joined together in a demonstration of more than three hundred people in downtown South Bend. In Goshen church-based groups called for a rally at the local courthouse on December 10, in conjunction with the nationally coordinated actions sponsored by United for Peace and Justice. Initially the county commissioners denied the group a permit, but this only helped to build interest in the protest.[34] More than 150 people turned out for the courthouse rally, while church groups collected contributions and relief items for humanitarian aid to Iraqi families.[35] Demonstrations also occurred in northern Indiana on Martin Luther King, Jr. day and then again on February 15, when hundreds of demonstrators turned out for rallies in South Bend, Elkhart, and Goshen. On March 8 nearly one hundred people gathered at the public library in South Bend for an International Women's Day event.

Protest action declined in the months after the invasion, but activists turned out again when Vice President Dick Cheney came to Notre Dame in October 2003. Many activists considered Cheney the chief architect of the war, the one who had most brazenly and repeatedly exaggerated the Iraqi weapons threat, and they decided to prepare an appropriate greeting. More than 150 people participated in a march and rally. The local WAND chapter helped to build the protest by conducting a search for weapons of mass destruction. Borrowing an idea from the Atlanta

Lois Nafziger, Karen Jacob, and Julia King from the Northern Indiana Chapter of Women's Action for New Directions searching for weapons of mass destruction, October 2003 (photo, Tim Nafziger).

chapter of WAND, thirty members of the group arrived at the rally wearing yellow haz-mat suits emblazoned with "hunt for WMD" fluorescent orange lettering. The group offered to help the vice president find those elusive weapons of mass destruction. The WAND action brought smiles from the participants and extensive news coverage from the media, especially television. The rally sent a message to the White House that even in the conservative heartland, administration officials could not expect to visit without facing antiwar protest.

Seattle has long been a center of progressive activism. The Puget Sound region had one of largest movements against the first Gulf War in 1990, and it witnessed a massive opposition campaign to the war in Iraq, as local groups formed a new coalition, Sound Nonviolent Opponents of War (SNOW).[36] Founded in September 2002, with office space and staff support provided by the Fellowship of Reconciliation, SNOW sought to build a broadly-based movement that could reach out to all sectors of society. The coalition eventually grew to encompass more than one hundred local and regional organizations.

Seattle organizers developed an innovative concept of neighborhood-based peace organizing. The idea emerged when Tom

Herriman in the community of Ballard invited neighbors within a three-block radius to a "cider press for peace." More than ninety people showed up, which was most of the neighborhood. They came not only to share a glass of cider, but also to meet neighbors who shared their concern about war in Iraq. The party was enjoyable, and helped to knit the neighborhood together. As word of the successful event spread, activists in the SNOW coalition saw the potential for a new model of antiwar organizing.

To develop the neighborhood approach, SNOW organized a mass meeting in early December at Garfield High School in central Seattle. The coalition vigorously promoted the event with mailings and posters in stores, churches, and offices throughout the city. More than 1,500 people filled the high school gymnasium.[37] Organizers placed signs and colored tape around the gym directing people to sit with others from their neighborhood. The event was a resounding success. The large turnout and the opportunity to meet like-minded people from their neighborhood energized participants. Within days of the Garfield event, potluck dinners were scheduled in dozens of communities, and neighbors began planning local education and action against war.

Eventually some seventy neighborhood peace groups formed in the Seattle area. They established their own coordinating committee and leadership group. The creation of this large, broadly-based network of neighborhood groups was unprecedented for the peace movement locally and nationally. It linked the local interest in connecting with neighbors to the broader global concern for preventing war. The neighborhood approach overcame the social isolation and sense of powerlessness that often inhibit activism. It made working against the war fun and fulfilling.[38]

Neighborhood groups and antiwar activists in Seattle developed a range of creative tactics. Some groups organized weekly vigils, often of a hundred or more people, at major traffic intersections. Among the homemade signs displayed at these vigils was the venerable "honk if you want peace," which invariably brought a cacophonous response. One group decided to display antiwar posters every Saturday on overpasses along Interstate 5, covering a stretch of more than one hundred miles from Seattle toward the Canadian border.[39] A drive along the busy highway created the impression of an entire community against war. A retired couple created bright red "No Iraq War" yard signs that sprouted in neighborhoods throughout the region and beyond. An estimated forty thousand yard signs appeared in the Puget Sound area, and more than one hundred thousand were distributed nationally.[40] Some groups organized local "conscientious projector" film showings. In February a newly formed veterans group organized a demonstration outside the home port of the U.S.S. *Turner Joy*, which was the ship involved in the infamous Gulf of Tonkin incident of 1964, prompting the congressional resolution that authorized war in Vietnam. When President Bush came to the city during the summer of 2003, local activists formed a "Billionaires for Bush" group. They rented a stretch limousine and carried signs that read "Because inequality isn't growing fast enough" and "The best president money can buy."

Seattle also witnessed more traditional forms of antiwar protest. On October 6, an estimated six to eight thousand people marched as part of the national day of protest sponsored by Not In Our Name.[41] Local church groups organized candlelight processions with hundreds of participants. On Martin Luther King, Jr. Day, hundreds of people marched to "support the poor and oppose the war." The February 15 demonstration was one of the largest antiwar actions ever held in that city. The crowd, which was estimated by organizers at fifty to sixty thousand and by the *Seattle Times* at twenty-eight thousand, stretched all the way through the city's downtown.[42] On the first day of the war in March, thousands of demonstrators gathered at the downtown federal building. They were met by a phalanx of Seattle police dressed in the menacing Darth Vader-like uniforms they had used during the November 1999 globalization protests. The police arrested several demonstrators and even ticketed passers-by when they honked to support the protest. The Seattle movement remained active after the invasion, although the number of neighborhood groups dwindled. SNOW and other groups continued to educate and demonstrate against the occupation of Iraq and for new directions in U.S. foreign and domestic policy.

The Pledge of Resistance

The Iraq antiwar movement featured a substantial campaign of direct action. The Iraq Pledge of Resistance, organized by Gordon Clark, former director of Peace Action, worked with a network of more than fifty local groups engaged in nationally coordinated civil disobedience against war. The campaign was modeled on the Central America Pledge of Resistance, which sponsored civil disobedience during the 1980s to prevent direct military intervention in Nicaragua and El Salvador.[43] The Iraq pledge was supported by the Fellowship of Reconciliation, Voices in the Wilderness, Pax Christi, Peace Action, and the War Resisters League, among other groups. The pledge sought to emulate the nonviolent witness of Gandhi and King, while also borrowing tactics from the global justice movement. Its political purpose, drawing from the Central America model, was to deter U.S. aggression by creating a credible threat of massive civil disobedience in the event of war. The hope was that this would convince decision makers to reconsider the costs of military action. Considerable resistance emerged, but the disruption never reached a scale where the theory could be tested. Nor was the campaign sufficiently large to serve as a credible deterrent. The Iraq pledge had few resources and little ability to shape local organizing strategies and decisions.

Most of the civil disobedience that occurred came in the days immediately after the outbreak of military hostilities in March. Some activists engaged in civil disobedience prior to the invasion—during the demonstrations on December 10 and then again during the King Day protests in mid-January—as a way of trying to prevent war through moral persuasion, but most concentrated on organizing resistance on the "day after." Organizers threatened to disrupt downtown business areas as a form of pressure to deter the war makers. In the week after war began, civil disobedience occurred in fifty cities, with thousands arrested.[44] In some of these actions, protesters halted traffic and blockaded government buildings. In Seattle demonstrators briefly blocked Interstate 5 in the center of the city. In Washington D.C. protesters attempted to block the Key Bridge. In New York civil resisters shut down a two-block stretch of Broadway. Most of these local actions were unconnected to the National Pledge of Resistance working group

The most significant actions occurred in Chicago and San Francisco. In Chicago more than ten thousand people gathered in Federal Plaza on Thursday night, March 21, the day after the outbreak of war. It was the largest antiwar rally in Chicago since the Vietnam era, and the crowd was in a defiant mood. After a spirited rally, the demonstrators began to move slowly toward the east, pushing the police line block by block toward Lake Shore Drive. A police officer later explained to a *Chicago Tribune* reporter that the only way to control "a crowd of that size" was to "move with it and try to contain it, not try to stop it."[45] When the crowd reached Lake Shore Drive, its numbers swelling, demonstrators snaked north onto Lake Shore Drive, blocking traffic in the northbound lane. When the demonstrators passed Navy Pier they took over the southbound lane as well. Protesters weaved in and out of stalled traffic. When part of the crowd pushed up Michigan Avenue and sat down on Chicago Avenue, the police moved in and began making arrests "by the busload." More than 550 protesters were arrested and held overnight. Another large rally was held in downtown Chicago the next day, but this time thousands of police in two lines surrounded the crowd. When the protesters headed up Dearborn Avenue, police lined the streets and refused to allow anyone to enter or leave the march. A smaller demonstration took place on Saturday, concluding three days of protest against war.

In San Francisco thousands of antiwar resisters converged on the city center March 21, shutting down thirty intersections and blockading a dozen buildings in the downtown financial district. The demonstrators used innovative hit and run tactics "to an extent never before seen in the Bay Area."[46] Small groups of activists armed with cell phones flitted from block to block, closing down intersections and then quickly dispersing as police arrived to make arrests. Some demonstrators chained themselves together, forcing police to use saws to separate them. The combination of mobile tactics and constant police action caused widespread chaos. The disruption was so severe that police were forced to ask motorists not to enter the downtown area. The police arrested 1,400 during the disturbances on Thursday.[47] A smaller but still angry crowd assembled the next day, but police kept a tighter rein on the demonstrators. Approximately two hundred were arrested on Friday.

The methods of urban lockdown and hit and run tactics would seem to be a far cry from the approaches of Gandhi and King, who encouraged their followers to engage in disciplined and orderly civil disobedience and to accept police arrest willingly and even joyfully. Yet there is no contradiction between the modern methods of the global justice movement, and some antiwar resisters, and the more traditional methods of Gandhi and King. It is sometimes necessary to generate what King called "creative tension" to expose injustices and force the political system to respond. In his classic study, *The Strategy of Social Protest*, William Gamson noted that political effectiveness sometimes depends on "the willingness to break rules and use non-institutional means . . . to use disruption as a strategy of influence."[48] Gamson found a direct correlation between disruption and political effectiveness. In their important book *Poor People's Movements*, Frances Fox Piven and Richard Cloward likewise saw a connection between political impact and the "disruptive effects" of mass defiance.[49] Disruption does not necessarily mean violence, however. Disruptive action can be counterproductive when it degenerates into vandalism and alienates third parties whose support is needed for political success.[50] Civil disobedience is most effective when it remains within a strictly nonviolent framework, which was most often the case in the Iraq campaign.

The concept of threatening mass civil disobedience as a deterrent to government action did not work in the case of Iraq, and generally seems a dubious strategy for social change. Some would question whether issuing threats, even if of a nonviolent nature, is compatible with the theory of democratic social change. One of the principal goals of nonviolent action is winning the support of third parties, seizing the moral high ground to achieve majority support. Writer/activist Barbara Deming was a proponent of nonviolent disruptive action, but she cautioned that such action must be done in a way "that the general population understands, that encourages more and more people to join us."[51] It is hard to see how the actions in Chicago, San Francisco, and other cities after the outbreak of war helped to win hearts and minds to the antiwar cause.

Proponents of mass civil disobedience point to the experiences of Vietnam and Central America as examples where government leaders refrained from military escalation out of concern for negative political consequences at home. The Nixon White House was indeed deeply worried about the disruptive impact of the antiwar movement (in its paranoia launching the Watergate operation that led to its undoing), and it tailored its war policies of Vietnamization and troop withdrawals to dampen mounting public opposition. In the case of Central America, military hard-liners in the Reagan administration would have preferred a larger and more decisive U.S. military commitment against the rebels in El Salvador and the Sandinista government in Nicaragua, but they opted for more covert and indirect measures (including the illegal Iran-Contra operation) to avoid greater political opposition at home.[52] While these leaders were concerned about antiwar disruption, there is no evidence that they reacted to the specific threat of organized civil disobedience. It would take a truly massive level of mobilization and commitment for such a threat to be credible. If such an organizing effort were possible, it would have greater impact if the action took place before the bombs started to fall rather than afterwards. Civil disobedience can be an effective, even necessary element of antiwar action, but it must be conducted in a way that wins public support, and that is preventive rather than reactive.

Communities of Color

"The most glaring weakness of the movement against the war in Iraq," wrote Barbara Epstein, "was the limited involvement of people of color, especially African Americans."[53] People of color were the most strongly opposed to war, but they were underrepresented among those who demonstrated against it. Opinion polls showed that blacks opposed the war in roughly the same percentages that whites supported it. A

Time/CNN poll of February 19–20, 2003 found 61 percent of blacks opposed to using military force against Saddam Hussein, compared to 35 percent among whites.[54] An ABC/*Washington Post* poll of February 26–March 2 found 62 percent of "nonwhites" in opposition to war, compared to 32 percent of whites.[55] Yet in most of the major national and regional protests the demonstrators were predominantly white. A major exception to this monochromatic pattern was the April 20, 2002 ANSWER-sponsored march in Washington, which attracted a very substantial turnout of Muslim Americans.[56] ANSWER generally did better than other antiwar coalitions in mobilizing people of color. African-Americans, Latinos and Arab Americans were part of the coalition's leadership, and ANSWER's political agenda of opposing racism and advocating Palestinian rights appealed more directly to the immediate concerns of communities of color. United for Peace and Justice was also relatively successful at attracting people of color. The February 15 rally in New York was fairly diverse racially, although it was not fully representative of New York's color composition.

According to Bob Wing, racial representation in the Iraq movement was better than in past antiwar movements.[57] Bill Fletcher agreed, noting that United for Peace and Justice responded positively to diversity concerns by reaching out to people of color.[58] The coalition also made a greater programmatic commitment to justice, including support for an equitable peace settlement between Israel and Palestine. The greater involvement of people of color also resulted from the Bush administration's policies, which combined a mobilization for war abroad with passage of the so-called Patriot Act and challenges to civil liberties at home. As some immigrant communities faced increased pressure, it was easier for many to see the links between militarism and racism. In keeping with its political agenda combining justice and peace issues, United for Peace and Justice made a concerted effort to develop a more racially diverse leadership structure. At its national conference in Chicago in June 2003, United for Peace and Justice elected a thirty-five-member steering committee that was perhaps the most diverse and broadly representative leadership group in peace movement history. More than half the members of the new steering committee were people of color, and nearly half were women.[59] This was a major advance for the antiwar movement.

The antiwar movement was less successful in attracting the participation of Latinos. The post September 11 crackdown on immigrants seriously affected Americans of Latin descent, especially the foreign born, and deterred many from speaking out publicly. Opinion polls nonetheless showed that Latinos were more opposed to war than Americans of European descent. An October 2002 poll by the Tomás Rivera Policy Institute in Claremont, California found 60 percent of Latinos opposed to war with Iraq.[60] Opposition to war was greatest among foreign-born Latinos. This skepticism toward invading Iraq was reflected in the unanimous vote of every Hispanic member of Congress against the resolution authorizing war. Yet few Latinos actively demonstrated against the war, and national antiwar groups made little effort to recruit them. Other than *War Times*, few antiwar publications were in Spanish. Win Without War made a belated effort to reach out to Latinos, but the effort came too late. In February I worked with Angela Sanbrano of CARECEN in Los Angeles and Arturo Gonzalez of the Willie Valesquez Institute in Texas to organize a "Latinos to Win Without War" group. A few national and regional leaders signed the initial statement, but the effort was cut short by the onset of war. The failure to involve a significant number of Latinos was a significant weakness of the antiwar movement. Hispanic Americans are becoming an increasingly important constituency in U.S. politics. If progressive activists hope to have influence on the direction of American political life, they will need a stronger presence in the Latino community.

The problem of inadequate racial diversity in the peace movement is a recurring one, and has been present in all the major campaigns in recent memory. The Vietnam antiwar movement, the Central America movement, the nuclear freeze campaign, the movement against the first Gulf War—all suffered from underrepresentation of communities of color. One of the dangers of this imbalance, Epstein noted, is that activists may attempt to address this problem by "slinging charges of racism at each other."[61] This has been a problem in past movements, and can have a corrosive effect on the morale and energy of activists. This was not a major problem in the Iraq antiwar movement, largely because the short amount of time available and the frenetic pace of activity did not provide much opportunity for self-flagellation. Although some charges of racism were raised within the movement, United for Peace and Justice responded effectively by taking concrete steps to create a more racially diverse leadership structure. Such attempts to broaden the racial representation of antiwar coalitions and organizations are important. Several traditional peace groups, including the American Friends Service Committee and Peace Action, have made major efforts over the years to create more racially diverse staffs and boards of directors. Within these groups, however, most of the members and local activists are white.

As antiwar groups have struggled to diversify, they have also recognized the importance of supporting the self-organization of blacks and other people of color.[62] During the Iraq movement and in previous antiwar campaigns, blacks and other groups have formed autonomous organizations to mobilize their communities. These initiatives do not oppose mainstream peace groups but offer alternative vehicles for articulating the specific concerns of people of color.[63] During the nuclear freeze campaign of the 1980s, when SANE and other groups struggled with issues of diversity, we sought the advice of Jack Odell, a member of our board of directors and former aide to Martin Luther King, Jr. Odell encouraged us to recruit blacks, Latinos, and Asians into our organizations, but he also urged us to support independent groups within these communities. Some people of color prefer to have their own organizations, he said, and want to frame the issues in ways that are most compelling to their constituency. Diverse groups can work in parallel within the movement, provided they strive toward the same ends, and show mutual respect and support for one another.

Although underrepresented at peace demonstrations, African-American, Latino, and other communities of color were by no means silent on the war. In Los Angeles and other California communities, Latino groups led protests against war and the clampdown on the rights of immigrants in the wake of September 11. In October 2002, some two hundred Mexican Americans signed an open letter to members of Congress urging opposition to the war resolution. The letter was read aloud at a rally in San Diego and published in several Latino papers. In January 2003, hundreds of Latinos joined an antiwar crowd of twenty thousand in Los Angeles. In March Latinos Por La Paz organized an antiwar vigil in Guadeloupe Plaza in Houston. African-American churches such as the Church of God in Christ and the Progressive National Baptists were among the first to register their opposition to war in Iraq. Many black leaders spoke out, including representative Barbara Lee (D-CA), who cast the lone vote in Congress against the resolution authorizing the use of force in Afghanistan; representatives Charles Rangel (D-NY) and John Conyers (D-MI), who spoke at the major antiwar rallies in Washington; Reverend Jesse Jackson, Sr., who spoke at several rallies in the United States and at the February 15 protest in London; and actor Danny Glover, chair of TransAfrica Forum. At the grassroots level Racial Justice 9-11 was formed as a network of antiwar groups. The network organized antiwar events in nearly a dozen cities in September 2002.[64] In Brooklyn, New York, Reverend Herbert Daughtry hosted large antiwar rallies at his House of the Lord church in November and January. In Washington, D.C., veteran organizer Damu Smith organized Black Voices for Peace, to help articulate African-American opposition to war.

These antiwar expressions are consistent with a long history of opposition to imperialism and military adventurism among African Americans and other communities of color. As authors Frances Beal and Ty dePass wrote in *The Black Scholar* in 1986:

> A consistent thread that has been woven into black intellectual and political thought in the United States has been a pattern of ardent anti-colonial and anti-imperialist consciousness. From a historical perspective, therefore, one of the strongest voices for peace within this country has come from the black community.[65]

People of color often have direct experience of institutional oppression and racism. They recognize more readily than most whites the connections between wars against people of color abroad and racism at home.[66] They are a natural constituency for peace and justice movements. Greater efforts to diversify antiwar activism can only strengthen the peace movement and increase the potential for preventing wars and military repression in the future.

Voices of Women

Women traditionally have been more vocally opposed to war than men and have been at the heart of many peace movements. Studies of public opinion have documented a substantial gender gap on war and military-related issues, with women consistently showing a greater propensity to support peaceful, diplomatic solutions to international crises and greater reluctance to endorse the use of military force.[67] The Iraq antiwar campaign was no exception, and in countless localities in the United States and throughout the world women took the lead in speaking out and organizing actions for peace. Opinion surveys during the Iraq debate showed that men were significantly more likely to favor war than women. An ABC/*Washington Post* poll of February 26–March 2 found 67 percent of men in favor of "war to remove Saddam Hussein," compared to only 51 percent of women.[68] A Zogby International poll of February 21 found 34 percent of men opposed to war, compared to 46 percent of women.[69] A March 3–8 poll commissioned by the Vietnam Veterans of America Foundation showed support for war at 53 percent among men but only 41 percent among women. Women were much more likely than men—54 percent compared to 34 percent—to favor giving UN weapons inspectors more time.[70]

Women's groups played important roles in national and local antiwar coalitions. Women religious orders contributed significantly to anti-

Code Pink demonstrators march in Washington, March 2003 (AP photo, Lisa Nipp).

war action. The National Organization for Women and WAND were leading groups within the Win Without War coalition. WAND helped to write and organize support for an extraordinary statement on the war from the National Council of Women's Organizations, a bipartisan network of more than 170 groups representing over seven million American women. The Council had not previously taken a stand on war and peace issues. Its January 15 statement emphasized the importance of diplomacy and nonviolent measures as "legitimate, effective and proven tools for diffusing and resolving conflict." It urged the government to focus on eliminating terrorism, arguing that a war in Iraq would not reduce that threat and might "increase hostility against the United States." It expressed "grave concern" about the heavy toll that war and increased military expenditures would exact on families, especially on women and children. The statement declared that the Council "opposes any preemptive military action against Iraq at this time."[71] The statement was published in *Ms* magazine, which included a special antiwar section in its winter 2003 issue.

Women activists also formed specific women's organizations to articulate a unique feminist peace perspective. In November 2002 a group of veteran peace and justice organizers led by Medea Benjamin, Starhawk, and Jodie Evans created Code Pink, Women for Peace. The goal, according to Benjamin, was to introduce a new discourse into a national debate dominated by the Bush administration's "testosterone-poisoned rhetoric."[72] The formation of Code Pink was announced at a vigil in front of the White House that began on November 17, 2002 and continued daily through March 8, 2003, International Women's Day. On that day ten thousand demonstrators marched toward the White House to protest the impending war. Women's Day actions also occurred in more than fifty cities in the United States. Across the country some ninety Code Pink chapters were formed.

The women's peace movement introduced a creative, at times humorous spirit into the antiwar debate. Liza Featherstone wrote in *The Nation* that Code Pink was "not an organization but a phenomenon: a sensibility reflecting feminist analysis and a campy playfulness influenced in style and philosophy both by ACT UP and the anti-globalization movement."[73] Code Pink specialized in high-spirited, disruptive actions that directly challenged those responsible for making and promoting the Bush administration's war policies. In November 2002 they interrupted Secretary of Defense Rumsfeld as he testified before Congress. In December they disrupted a briefing by State Department public relations official Charlotte Beers, unfurling a banner that read, "Charlotte, stop selling war." One of their trademark actions was to deliver "You're fired" pink slips, presenting actual women's slips to officials who supported the war. Among those targeted for such treatment was New York senator Hillary Rodham Clinton. The Code Pink actions were part of a rising tide of innovative feminist action against war. Early in January 2003 a group of women gathered on the beach in Point Reyes, California to spell out "Peace" with their nude bodies. The women explained that they were protesting the Bush administration's "naked aggression."

Another creative women's initiative was the Lysistrata Project. Organized by actresses and women involved in the theatre in New York and Los Angeles, the project sought to bring to light the powerful but mirthful message of the 2,400-year-old antiwar comedy by Aristophanes. The story of Lysistrata (literally "she who disbands armies") tells of

Athenian and Spartan women who refused to sleep with their men until they ceased their warring ways. On March 3, 2003 an estimated one thousand readings of the play took place in all fifty states and in fifty-nine countries.[74] In New York and Los Angeles, prominent actresses and actors headlined star performances. In London hundreds of British actresses and actors gathered at 11:00 a.m. in Parliament Square to read the play in what they termed a mass Greek chorus of disapproval.

The multiple, diverse forms of action traced here were unable to prevent war, but they had enduring impacts. Many of the movement's criticisms of war were proven correct when U.S. forces failed to find weapons of mass destruction and Iraq degenerated into chaos. Skepticism about the consequences of war deepened in the media and in society. Antiwar coalitions remained active in numerous countries, as polls showed continued global opposition to U.S. military policy. Many of the groups and coalitions that formed in the U.S. continued to speak out against the doctrine of unilateral preemption and the military occupation of Iraq. Within mainstream organizations—from church denominations to women's groups—the legacy of the antiwar debate persisted in continuing doubts about Bush administration policy. Local groups remained active, although diminished in scale, and raised a continuing voice for peace. Social movements do not disappear when their immediate cause for mobilization passes. They may shrink in size, and like a whale may slip below the surface for a time, but they remain alive in the form of organizations and networks, and may rise again to the surface as opportunities and conditions allow.

Notes

1. Glenn Kessler and Mike Allen, "Bush Faces Increasingly Poor Image Overseas," *Washington Post*, 24 February 2003, A01; CNN, "Poll: U.S. More a Threat Than Iraq," 11 February 2003, <http://edition.cnn.com/2003/WORLD/europe/02/11/british.survey> (accessed 19 November 2003).

2. Stefaan Walgrave and Joris Verhulst, "The February 15 Worldwide Protests Against a War in Iraq: An Empirical Test of Transnational Opportunities," (unpublished paper, University of Antwerp, 2003).

3. Crowd estimates in this paragraph drawn from Bill Weinberg, "Antiwar Around the World," Global Movement Against War: Taking it to the Streets, *Nonviolent Activist* 20, no. 2 (March-April 2003): 5, 9. See also Norm Dixon, "The Largest Coordinated Antiwar Protest in History," *Scoop* [New Zealand] 20 February 2003, <http://www.scoop.co.nz/mason/archive/scoop/stories/ed/fa/200302201002.43a56c8a.html> (accessed 14 November 2003).

4. Steve Cobble, e-mail message to author, 14 December 2003.

5. Tekla Szymanski, "Schröder Beats Bush in German Election," *World Press Review* (26 September 2002), <http://www.worldpress.org/europe/741.cfm> (accessed 19 November 2003).

6. Philip P. Pan, "Turkey Rejects U.S. Use of Bases," *Washington Post*, 2 March 2003, A1.

7. CNN, "NATO Approves Turkish Deployment," 20 February 2003, <http://www.cnn.com/2003/WORLD/meast/02/19/sprj.irq.nato.turkey/index.html> (accessed 19 November 2003).

8. Percentages of opposition to military action in Iraq are as follows: U.S.—30 percent, U.K.—51 percent, Italy—81 percent, Spain—81 percent, Poland—73 percent, Germany—69 percent, and Turkey—86 percent. Responses are from polling conducted by the Pew Global Attitudes Project March 10-17, 2003. Respondents in the U.K., Italy, Spain, and Poland were asked, "Would you favor or oppose [survey country] joining the U.S. and other allies in military action in Iraq to end Saddam Hussein's rule?" In the U.S. the question posed was, "Would you favor or oppose taking military action in Iraq to end Saddam Hussein's rule?" In Germany and Turkey respondents were asked, "Would you favor or oppose the U.S. and other allies taking military action in Iraq to end Saddam Hussein's rule?" The Pew Global Attitudes Project, "America's image further erodes, Europeans want weaker ties: But post-war Iraq will be better off, most say," March 18, 2003. Polling conducted and reported by the Pew Research Center for the People & the Press. Available at the *Pew Global Attitudes Project* <http://www.people-press.org> (accessed November 13, 2003).

9. BBC, "Australian PM Censured over Iraq," 5 February 2003, <http://news.bbc.co.uk/2/low/asia-pacific/2727551.stm> (accessed 19 November 2003).

10. *Guardian* (London), "Boost for Religious Parties in Pakistan Elections," 11 October 2002,<http://www.guardian.co.uk/pakistan/Story/0,2763,810103,00.html> (accessed 21 November 2003).

11. Jimmy Carter, "Just War—or a Just War?," *New York Times*, 9 March 2003.

12. For a view of churches in the nuclear freeze movement, see chapter by the author, "God Against the Bomb," in David Cortright, *Peace Works: The Citizen's Role in Ending the Cold War* (Boulder, Colo.: Westview Press, 1993), 40–60.

13. Barbara Epstein, "Notes on the Antiwar Movement," *Monthly Review* 55, no. 3 (July-August 2003): 115.

14. BBC, "Pope Condemns War in Iraq," 13 January 2003, <http://news.bbc.co.uk/1/hi/world/europe/2654109.stm> (accessed 24 November 2003).

15. CBC, "Pope Says War Threatens Humanity," 22 March 2003, <http://www.cbc.ca/stories/2003/03/22/popewar_030322> (accessed 24 November 2003).

16. Quoted in "Without Disarmament, Peace is Disarmed, says Archbishop Martino," *ZENIT,* 17 December 2002, <http://zenit.org/english/visualizza.phtml?sid=29125> (accessed 2 December 2003); and Gerard O'Connell, "Bullets in Iraq, But all Quiet on the Vatican Front," *Our Sunday Visitor*, 13 April 2003, <http://www.osvpublishing.com/periodicals/show-article.asp?pid=793> (accessed 2 December 2003).

17. Statement of Cardinal Joseph Ratzinger, 21 September 2002, <http://www.usccb.org/bishops/iraq.htm> (accessed 29 December 2003).

18. Gerard Powers, interview by author, 29 December 2003.

19. Bob Edgar, interview by author, 27 August 2003.

20. Mark LeVine, "The Peace Movement Plans for the Future," *Middle East Report* (July 2003), <http://www.merip.org/mero/interventions/levine_interv.html> (accessed 24 November 2003).

21. Rebecca Solnit, "Acts of Hope: Challenging Empire on the World Stage," *Orion* (20 May 2003), <http://www.oriononline.org/pages/oo/sidebars/Patriotism/index_SolnitPR.html> (accessed 24 November 2003).

22. Remarks by Bob Muehlenkamp, co-convener, U.S. Labor Against War, 26 April 2003 meeting, Chicago, Illinois, <http://www.uslaboragainstwar.org> (accessed 16 September 2003).

23. AFL-CIO Executive Council, "Iraq," 27 February 2003, <http://www.aflcio.org/aboutaflcio/ecouncil/ec02272003h.cfm> (accessed 16 September 2003).

24. Edith Kaplan, "A Hundred Peace Movements Bloom," *The Nation* (6 January 2003), <http://www.thenation.com/doc.mhtml?i=20030106&s=kaplan> (accessed 18 December 2003).

25. See the Not In Our Name website,<http://www.notinourname.net/about.html> (accessed 19 August 2003).

26. Demonstration estimates drawn from the Not In Our Name website, <http://www.notinourname.net/reports.html> (accessed 19 August 2003).

27. The ad appeared in the *New York Times* on 26 September 2002. Among the signers were John J. Mearsheimer and Robert Pape, University of Chicago; Robert Jervis and Kenneth N. Waltz, Columbia University; and Stephen M. Walt, Harvard University.

28. William J. Broad, "41 Nobel Laureates Sign Declaration Against a War Without International Support," *New York Times*, 28 January 2003, A12.

29. Karin Simonson, "The Anti-war Movements: Waging Peace on the Brink of War," Paper prepared for the Programme on NGOs and Civil Society of the Centre for Applied Sciences in International Negotiation, March 2003, <http://www.casin.ch/pdf/The%Anti-War"20Movement.pdf> (accessed 10 December 2003).

30. Estimates from the National Youth and Student Peace Coalition website, <http://www.nyspc.net/home.html> (accessed 21 November 2003).

31. Statement of Karen Dolan, Director, Cities for Peace, National Conference of the Rainbow/PUSH Coalition, 24 June 2003, Chicago, Illinois.

32. George A. Lopez, "Iraq and Just War Thinking," *Commonweal* CXXIX, no. 16 (27 September 2002), <http://www.commonwealmagazine.org/> (accessed 29 December 2003).

33. Karen Jacob, interview by author, 28 December 2003.

34. David Fast, interview by author, 8 December 2003.

35. Amber Brockway, "Goshen Rally Opposes War with Iraq," *Goshen News*, 11 December 2002, A1.

36. Mike Yarrow, interview by author, 20 December 2003.

37. Monica Soto, "Antiwar Protest Packs Garfield High Gym," *Seattle Times*, 9 December 2002, <http://archives.seattletimes.nwsource.com/cgi-bin/texis.cgi/web/vortex/display?slug=protest09&date=20021209> (accessed 27 December 2003).

38. Yarrow, interview.

39. "One Hundred Miles of Protest and Growing," *NorthWest Citizen* (Bellingham), 4 January 2003, <http://nwcitizen.us/usa/overpass/jan4gallery/jan4.htm> (accessed 27 December 2003).

40. Yarrow, interview.

41. Jennifer Langston, "Thousands Walk for Peace," *Seattle Post-Intelligencer*, 7 October 2002, <http://seattlepi.nwsource.com/local/90107_peace07.shtml> (accessed 27 December 2003).

42. J. Patrick Coolican, "Crowd Count Adds up to Infinite Interpretation," *Seattle Times*, 17 February 2003, <http://archives.seattletimes.nwsource.com/cgi-bin/texis.cgi/web/vortex/display?slug=crowdsize17e&date=20030217> (accessed 27 December 2003).

43. Ken Butigan, "The Pledge of Resistance: Lessons from a Movement of Solidarity and Nonviolent Direct Action," <http://www.peacepledge.org/resist/lessons.shtm> (accessed 21 November 2003).

44. Report of Gordon Clark, "Iraq Pledge of Resistance," 28 March 2003, <http://www.peacepledge.org/resist/march282003.shtm> (accessed 24 November 2003).

45. Sean D. Hamill and David Heinzmann, "Chicago Anti-War Demonstration Shuts Down City," *Chicago Tribune*, 21 March 2003, <http://www.why-war.com/news/author.php?name=Sean+D.+Hamill+and+David+Heinzmann> (accessed 1 December 2003).

46. Joe Garofoli and Jim Herron Zamora, "San Francisco Police Play Catch Up; Protestors Roam," *San Francisco Chronicle*, 21 March 2003.

47. CNN, "Hundreds of Thousands Protest War," 22 March 2003, <http://www.cnn.com/2003/US/03/21/sprj.irq.protests/> (accessed 1 December 2003).

48. William Gamson, *The Strategy of Social Protest*, 2d ed. (Belmont, Calif.: Wadsworth Publishing, 1990), 156.

49. Frances Fox Piven and Richard A. Cloward, *Poor People's Movements: Why They Succeed, How They Fail* (New York: Vintage Books, 1979), 24.

50. See the author's discussion of these issues in "The Power of Nonviolence," *The Nation* 274, no. 6 (18 February 2002).

51. Barbara Deming, "On the Necessity to Liberate Minds," in *We Are All Part of One Another: A Barbara Deming Reader*, ed. Jane Meyerding (Philadelphia: New Society Publishers, 1984), 199.

52. See the author's discussion of these developments in *Peace Works: The Citizen's Role in Ending the Cold War* (Boulder, Colo.: Westview Press, 1993), 221–234.

53. Epstein, "Notes on the Antiwar Movement," 111.

54. Polling Report, "Iraq (p. 4)," conducted by Harris Interactive, <http://www.pollingreport.com/iraq4.htm> (accessed 28 August 2003).

55. Polling Report, "Iraq (p. 4)," fieldwork by TNS Intersearch, <http://www.pollingreport.com/iraq4.htm> (accessed 28 August 2003).

56. Libero Della Piana, "War's Racial Edge," *ColorLines* (Spring 2003): 21.

57. Bob Wing, interview by author, 14 November 2003.

58. Bill Fletcher, interview by author, 16 December 2003.

59. For a full report on the conference see the United for Peace and Justice press release of 15 June 2003, <http://www.unitedforpeace.org/article.php?id=1882> (accessed 11 December 2003).

60. Poll results available at the Tomás Rivera Policy Institute, <http://www.trpi.org/press/102902.html> (accessed 1 December 2003).

61. Epstein, "Notes on the Antiwar Movement," 112.

62. Epstein, "Notes on the Antiwar Movement," 112.

63. Della Piana, "War's Racial Edge."

64. Tomio Geron, "Racial Justice Groups Organize Against War," *War Times* 6, October 2002, <http://www.war-times.org/issues/6art9.html> (accessed 24 November 2003).

65. Frances Beal and Ty dePass, "The Historical Black Presence in the Struggle for Peace," *The Black Scholar* (17 January/February 1986): 2.

66. Della Piana, "War's Racial Edge."

67. For a detailed social science analysis of this phenomenon, see Richard C. Eichenberg, "Gender Differences in Public Attitudes toward the Use of Force by the United States, 1990-2003," *International Security* 28, no. 1 (Summer 2003): 110-141.

68. Polling Report, "Iraq (p. 4)," Harris Interactive.

69. "Aggregate Zogby America Pre War Support, 9/25/02 thru 3/17/03," Zogby International, special report to Fourth Freedom Forum, 26 August 2003.

70. Greenberg Quinlan Rosner Research Inc., "Public Supports Bush, is More Divided Over Iraq: Report on the First WorldView Survey for VVAF," memorandum from Jeremy Rosner and William McInturff to Vietnam Veterans of America Foundation, 14 March 2003, <http://www.greenbergresearch.com/publications/reports/VVAF031403_m.pdf> (accessed 28 August 2003).

71. "National Council of Women's Organizations Statement on the War with Iraq," National Council of Women's Organizations, 15 January 2003, <http://www.now.org/issues/global/031103ncwo.html> (accessed 1 December 2003).

72. Quoted in Ann Moline, "'Code Pink' White House Vigil Continues," National Organization for Women, 29 December 2002, <http://www.now.org/eNews/dec2002/122902peace.html> (accessed 24 November 2003).

73. Liza Featherstone, "Mighty in Pink," *The Nation* (3 March 2003), <http://www.thenation.com/doc.mhtml?i=20030303&s=featherstone> (accessed 18 December 2003).

74. Figures from Lysistrata Project report, <http://www.pecosdesign.com/lys/archive.html> (accessed 21 November 2003).

Chapter Four

Communicating
for Peace

The Iraq antiwar movement featured the largest and most sophisticated media communications effort in the history of the peace movement. Antiwar movements in the past have suffered from poor media relations. As Todd Gitlin and others have observed, peace activists have been slow to recognize the strategic significance of crafting and delivering effective messages. During the Vietnam era the image of the peace movement was often that of a motley and anarchic rabble. The major coalitions involved were more interested in street protests than media communications, and little effort was made to hire professional media consultants or sponsor public relations and advertising campaigns. When the Nixon administration misrepresented the movement as violent, issuing its disingenuous call for "law and order," antiwar activists were unable to mount an effective reply. Partly as a result, public support for the peace movement declined, even as antiwar sentiment generally increased. In recent decades, peace and justice activists have come to recognize the power and influence of the media. They have seen how communications strategies are becoming the dominant factor in shaping political discourse and swaying political opinion. When the debate over war in Iraq began, many activists were determined to mount an effective public relations and media communications campaign.

Social movements face enormous challenges in gaining news coverage. Unlike prominent political leaders, they cannot simply call a press conference and expect the media to report what they say. As Charlotte Ryan and other media analysts have observed, challenger groups seldom have the resources to match the communications power of government, especially when the adversary is the White House. Activists also must contend with the inherent media bias in favor of those in power—a bias that is particularly pronounced on national security issues.[1] The options available to challenger groups for overcoming these obstacles are limited. They can organize events that attract media coverage, they can place advertisements that communicate their message directly, or they can use celebrities and "famous faces" to attract publicity to their cause. The Iraq antiwar movement used all of these methods, and was generally successful at each.

The February 15 demonstrations in the U.S. and around the world were enormously successful in attracting media coverage. They were the most visible news-creating events of the entire Iraq movement. The demonstrations that day were the lead story in practically every broadcast and print news source in the United States and in much of the world. Never before had the peace movement attracted so much press coverage. The image of the antiwar movement as a superpower was the direct result of the February demonstrations and the resulting media coverage. The demonstrations conveyed a simple "no to war" message that was easily understood and resonated well with world opinion. The demonstrations were dramatic "real world events" that generated unprecedented news coverage and helped to influence public opinion and policy. They conferred credibility and legitimacy on the antiwar cause. By contrast, the earlier demonstrations sponsored by ANSWER and Not In Our Name were less effective in generating positive news coverage. These groups paid less attention to media relations, conveyed a more complex message, and sometimes employed language that may have resonated well with radical activists but had little meaning for average citizens.

Although much smaller in scale than the United for Peace and Justice demonstrations, the actions of Code Pink were also successful in generating favorable media coverage. The women activists were a nettlesome presence at appearances of war-making officials, and thus became the subject of press coverage. By using feminist language and symbols, and by employing disruptive theatrics, Code Pink activists attracted considerable press attention and helped to frame opposition to war as a special concern of women.

One of the most important dimensions of media strategy is the framing of messages. Every political contest is at its core a struggle over the meaning of words and ideas. Social change often hinges on the way in which messages are interpreted and packaged. The context in which a message is delivered is often more important than the specific message itself. According to William Gamson, the images and metaphors activists convey are central to their prospects for political success.[2] Ideas such as justice or peace do not exist in a vacuum, in some rarified form that everyone automatically accepts. Their meaning is shaped by the social and political context in which they are communicated. Activists increasingly understand that they must shape that context and offer compelling images, symbols, and metaphors that resonate with and

Working Assets sponsored billboard in Detroit (photo, Working Assets).

capture public imagination. The contest over symbolic expression has become a crucial element of social movement struggle.

Win Without War was specifically created as a vehicle for media communications. The coalition placed a great deal of emphasis on the framing of its message and the maintenance of a sustained and disciplined press operation. From the outset Win Without War sought to portray itself as mainstream and patriotic. Its press releases and newspaper ads featured an American flag, and its mission statement began with "We are patriotic Americans. . . ." By framing its message in patriotic terms, Win Without War sought to capture the flag and thereby inoculate itself against the usual charges of aiding the enemy. The coalition explicitly condemned Saddam Hussein's rule, and supported vigorous inspections and containment as alternative means of countering the Iraqi dictator. The coalition expressed full support for international efforts to combat terrorism, although it was careful to avoid any specific reference to the administration's "war on terror" (so as not to reinforce Bush's militarized metaphor and policies). Through the framing and delivery of these patriotic messages, Win Without War sought to reach the political mainstream and effectively contest the Bush administration's case for war.

There was considerable, sometimes heated debate within the movement about the use of patriotic symbols and language. Some activists expressed discomfort with the traditional militaristic meaning of the flag. As George Lakoff and other communications experts noted, right wing groups had "commandeered patriotic language" and appropriated the meaning of the flag and other national emblems.[3] Many activists argued that a patriotic frame was necessary both on principle and as a pragmatic means of winning the acceptance and support of persuadable Americans. The peace movement should not concede patriotism to militarism, they insisted, but should struggle to redefine the concept of loving one's country. The problem has been that many people confuse patriotism and nationalism. Patriotism implies positive values of sacrifice, duty, honor, selflessness, and generosity toward others. Nationalism, by contrast, evokes images of domination, militarism, xenophobia, and imperialism. The challenge is to emphasize the former over the latter. This means engaging in message framing contests to assert the meaning of commonly used words and images. Many activists attempted to redefine patriotism by pointing to the positive elements of America's role in the world—support for human rights, aid for the poor, and U.S. participation in the United Nations and other international institutions. They also insisted that the greatness of America lies in core values—freedom, democracy, and opportunity—not in war and militarism. They tried to send a message that "peace is patriotic" by displaying the flag and other patriotic symbols as part of the movement's visual imagery.

Working Assets president Michael Kieschnick was one of those who sought to reclaim patriotic themes. "We are trying to take back the language," said Kieschnick.[4] Peace activists are just as patriotic as war supporters, he insisted. Working Assets placed hundreds of billboards and advertising signs in San Francisco, Washington D.C., New York, and other cities with the message "Support Our Troops. Bring Them Home Now." Activists criticized the Bush administration's funding cuts for low-ranking service members and veterans, and demanded increased pay and benefits for those who serve. This was a form of political jui jitsu, as antiwar activists outflanked war advocates in expressing support for men and women in uniform.

Working Assets also attempted to link patriotism and energy conservation, emphasizing the national interest in weaning the U.S. economy from dependence on Middle East oil. On the day of the January 18, 2003 rally in San Francisco, more than five thousand Working Assets customers and friends attended an "Environmentalists Against the War" rally at the steps of Grace Cathedral. The Sierra Club joined in cosponsoring the event. Afterwards, an eco-caravan of one hundred hybrid and electric cars proceeded down to the main protest rally. Bumper stickers on the vehicles read "Go Solar, Not Ballistic" and "Real Patriots Drive Hybrids." Activists in many parts of the country agreed on the need to emphasize patriotic messages and found creative ways of linking their love for country and planet with opposition to war.

The Win Without War name was itself a form of message framing. The phrase was alliterative and easy to express. It conveyed a positive theme (everyone wants to "win") without the negativity of being "against" war or the military. Yet it was specific about seeking a solution "without war," thus marking a clear break with the position of the Bush administration. The title implied support for constructive alternatives to war, such as vigorous UN weapons inspections and continued containment. It conveyed a desire to win the face-off with Saddam Hussein through diplomatic rather than military means. It also implied a strategy for winning the struggle against Al Qaeda, through the force of law rather than the law of force. The name avoided the ambiguity and negative connotation that some people, still influenced by cold war misconceptions, associate with the traditional "peace" movement. Win Without War projected a new, proactive image for the antiwar movement. It was both message and sound bite, and it became a brand that was the most widely communicated message of the movement.[5]

Advertising

The Win Without War coalition launched a substantial public relations and media advertising effort to communicate its message. The media firm Fenton Communications played a central role in this effort, through its special "antiwar room" media project. The project provided sustained professional public relations services, helped to frame messages, and developed media communications strategies. It contacted hundreds of reporters and editors every week, organized numerous press events, booked spokespersons on national and regional interview programs, and placed paid newspaper and television advertising throughout the country. Other movement media firms also played an important role in communicating the antiwar message, including Mainstream Media in California, and Avenging Angels in New York.

The Win Without War media strategy sought to raise doubts about invading Iraq among persuadable voters. Opinion polls in early 2003 showed approximately one-third of the population strongly opposed to war, with about 60 percent favoring military action. When the question of UN authorization was added, support for unilateral war dropped below 40 percent. This left a sizeable swing group in the middle that shifted back and forth depending on the flow of events and the public debate. After the president's State of the Union address in late January 2003 and Secretary of State Powell's subsequent report to the UN Security Council in early February, support for a military invasion increased, as some

Public Responses to Standard Polling Questions during the Weeks before the War

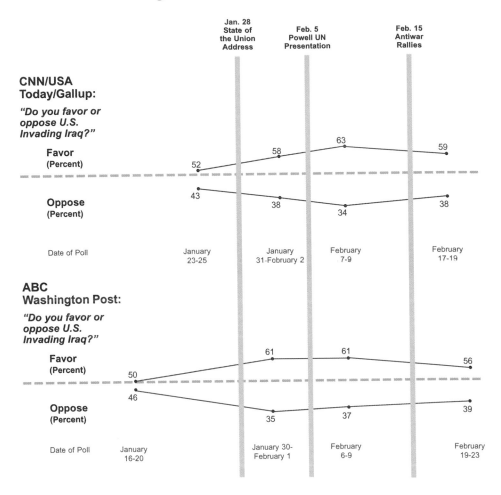

undecided citizens were persuaded to support the president. After the February 15 antiwar rallies and the virtual march eleven days later, the so-called "Powell bounce" faded.[6] Polls showed a slight decline in support for war, as persuadable voters shifted more to the opposition. The movement's mobilizing and media efforts seemed to have a measurable impact on public opinion.

The political debate about the war was a struggle to influence the persuadable middle. The movement's use of mainstream messages and patriotic symbolism was a conscious attempt to influence this swing opinion. So was the movement's emphasis on supporting UN weapons inspections and its insistence on gaining Security Council authorization for any military action in Iraq. The movement was successful in winning support for its position, especially in the weeks immediately prior to the invasion in late February and early March 2003. Opinion surveys found a majority of respondents opposed to a war fought without UN authorization. An *LA Times* poll of January 30–February 2 found 65 percent of respondents agreeing that the U.S. should take military action "only if it has the support of the UN Security Council."[7] A *Newsweek* poll of February 6–7 asked respondents if they would support war "if the U.S. acted alone, without the support of the UN." Thirty-seven percent indicated support but 59 percent were opposed.[8] Opinion surveys also found substantial support for continued UN weapons inspections.[9] The movement's "inspections, not war" message and advocacy of UN authorization sought to undermine support for Bush's unilateral war policy.

Antiwar groups spent approximately $2 million on newspaper and television advertising in the months leading up to the U.S. attack. The ads were a means of guaranteeing that the antiwar message was heard. They assured that the movement's words and images were communicated directly as intended, without mediation or interpretation. At times the advertising efforts were themselves a news story and helped to generate "earned media" through the novelty and sharply worded focus of the message. One of the boldest ads, produced by Fenton Communications, appeared in the *New York Times* on September 25, 2002 under the banner "Uncle oSama Wants You to Invade Iraq." The ad featured Osama bin Laden in the traditional Uncle Sam pose urging Washington to "Go ahead. Send me a new generation of recruits. Your bombs will fuel hatred of America and their desire for revenge. Please attack Iraq. Distract yourself from attacking Al Qaeda. Go ahead. . . . Make my day." The provocative ad generated dozens of news stories, was widely reproduced around the world, and was read on the floor of the U.S. Senate.

Another controversial and innovative ad was a thirty-second television spot produced by MoveOn in January 2003. The ad reproduced the famous "Daisy" ad from the 1964 presidential campaign of Lyndon Johnson: a girl innocently picks petals from a daisy as a voice ominously counts down to zero, and the screen dissolves into a nuclear mushroom cloud. The ad was an attempt to counter the Bush administration's disingenuous use of the mushroom cloud image. The president and his national security adviser Condoleezza Rice said on several occasions that the United States could not wait for hard evidence of Saddam's weapons threat because the smoking gun everyone was seeking could end up being a nuclear mushroom cloud. Spinmeisters in the White House obviously cooked up the phrase and had it inserted into key speeches

Paid for by MoveOn.org

The "daisy ad," fashioned after the famous Lyndon Johnson television spot from the 1964 presidential campaign (photo, MoveOn).

and television appearances. The MoveOn ad reversed the image and sent a message that, if Saddam Hussein actually had such weapons, the war itself could lead to their use. The ad stirred further controversy and attracted media attention to the antiwar campaign of MoveOn and other groups.

True Majority and Business Leaders for Sensible Priorities also mounted an extensive advertising campaign, drawing upon the talent of Gene Case and Avenging Angels. Case had worked for the Lyndon Johnson campaign in 1964 and was a founding partner of Jordan McGrath Case and Partners, a $500 million-a-year public relations company. In October 2002 Business Leaders for Sensible Priorities placed a full-page ad in the *New York Times* with the banner, "They're selling war. We're not buying." In December 2002 the business executives joined with religious leaders in appealing to Bush: "Jesus changed your heart. Let him change your mind." In January 2003 Business Leaders for Sensible Priorities placed a full-page ad in the *Wall Street Journal* signed by Republican Party supporters and donors. The January ad was written and paid for by Edward H. Hamm, a member of the Republican Regents, a committee of donors who contribute six figures or more to the party. The ad was entitled "A Republican Dissent on Iraq" and proclaimed in bold print, "a billion bitter enemies will rise out of this war." True Majority also produced a series of television ads that paired foreign policy experts with Hollywood

I WANT YOU
TO INVADE IRAQ

Go ahead. Send me a new generation of recruits. Your bombs will fuel their hatred of America and their desire for revenge. Americans won't be safe anywhere. Please, attack Iraq. Distract yourself from fighting Al Qaeda. Divide the international community. Go ahead. Destabilize the region. Maybe Pakistan will fall – we want its nuclear weapons. Give Saddam a reason to strike first. He might draw Israel into a fight. Perfect! So please – invade Iraq. Make my day.

TomPaine.common sense

Osama says: 'I Want You to Invade Iraq.'
TomPaine.com *features reasons why we shouldn't.*

© 2002 The Florence Fund, PO Box 53303, Washington, DC 20009 artists and popular musicians. One ad featured actress Susan Sarandon with retired admiral Jack Shanahan. The television spots were placed nationally and in targeted local markets. Other organizations that placed full-page ads in the *New York Times* included Not In Our Name, the Center for Community Change, and 1199 Service Employees' International Union, New York's Health Care Union. Actor Sean Penn placed a full-page ad in the *Washington Post* in October. As noted earlier, Sojourners announced its six-point plan with full-page ads in all the major London dailies in March.

Artists Unite

The antiwar media effort was greatly aided by the development of Artists United to Win Without War, which was formed in December 2002, and Musicians United to Win Without War, which emerged in February 2003. The artists committee was initiated by actor Mike Farrell and producer/director Robert Greenwald after a Los Angeles briefing/ reception featuring former UN weapons inspector Scott Ritter in early October 2002. Farrell had contacted me in July to inquire about experts on the Iraq issue. He said that artists were becoming increasingly concerned about the threat of war, but wanted to be educated. Was Iraq really a threat? Is military action necessary? As Farrell put it, "Our career depends on our reputation and our credibility. We're not foreign policy experts. We need to be sure of our information before speaking out." Several weeks later, I called to suggest a briefing for the Hollywood community and Farrell agreed. The October 2 session was held at the home of Stanley K. Sheinbaum, philanthropist, economist, former University of California regent, and longtime progressive leader for civil rights and peace. Dozens of artists and Los Angeles community leaders came to Sheinbaum's home that evening, including Warren Beatty, Annette Benning, Barbra Streisand, James Brolin, and James Cromwell. Ritter gave a riveting and authoritative presentation, based on his personal experience as a Marine Corps officer during the first Gulf War and seven years as a senior UN weapons inspector in Iraq. He and Gulf War vet Erik Gustafson gave exactly the kind of informed reassurance that Farrell and Greenwald were seeking. After the session we huddled to discuss next steps. Ritter suggested asking a few actors to sign a statement as a way of attracting press attention. Greenwald was skeptical: "no one will sign, the press won't cover it." He and Farrell had been opposed to creating a new organization, but the presentations that evening were powerful and convincing, and they agreed to give it a try.

KEEP AMERICA SAFE

Artists Say
Win Without War

War talk in Washington is alarming and unnecessary.

We are patriotic Americans who share the belief that Saddam Hussein cannot be allowed to possess weapons of mass destruction. We support rigorous United Nations weapons inspections to assure Iraq's effective disarmament.

However, a preemptive military invasion of Iraq will harm American national interests. Such a war will increase human suffering, arouse animosity toward our country, increase the likelihood of terrorist attacks, damage the economy, and undermine our moral standing in the world. It will make us less, not more, secure.

We reject the doctrine—a reversal of long-held American tradition—that our country, alone, has the right to launch first-strike attacks.

The valid U.S. and U.N. objective of disarming Saddam Hussein can be achieved through legal diplomatic means. There is no need for war. Let us instead devote our resources to improving the security and well being of people here at home and around the world.

Signed,

Artists United to Win Without War

Mike Farrell and Robert Greenwald, Co-Chairs	Matt Damon	Samaria Graham	Dave Matthews	Susan Sarandon
	Dana Daurey	Robert Greenwald	Kent McCord	William Schallert
Gillian Anderson	Ambassador Jonathan Dean (U.S. Rep. to NATO-Warsaw Pact)	Robert Guillaume	Robert Duncan McNeill	Tony Shalhoub
Edward Asner		Paul Haggis	Mike Mills (REM)	Jack Shanahan, Vice Adm. U.S. Navy (Ret.)
Rene Auberjonois	Jonathan Demme	Robert David Hall	Janel Moloney	
David Bale	Vincent D'Onofrio	Ethan Hawke	Esai Morales	Martin Sheen
Kim Basinger	David Duchovny	Ken Howard	Ed O'Neill	Armin Shimerman
Ed Begley, Jr.	Olympia Dukakis	Helen Hunt	Chris Noth	Gloria Steinem
Theo Bikel	Charles S. Dutton	Anjelica Huston	Peter Onorati	Marcia Strassman
Barbara Bosson	Hector Elizondo	LaTanya Richardson Jackson	Alexandra Paul	Michael Stipe (REM)
Jackson Browne	Cary Elwes	Samuel L. Jackson	Ambassador Edward Peck (former U.S. Ambassador to Iraq)	Susan Sullivan
Peter Buck (REM)	Shelley Fabares	Jane Kaczmarek		Loretta Swit
Diahann Carroll	Mike Farrell	Melina Kanakaredes	Seth Peterson	Studs Terkel
Eugene J. Carroll, Jr., Rear Adm. U.S. Navy (Ret.)	Mia Farrow	Casey Kasem	CCH Pounder	Lily Tomlin
	Laurence Fishburne	Mimi Kennedy	David Rabe	Blair Underwood
Kathleen Chalfant	Sean Patrick Flanery	Barbara Kopple	Alan Rachins	Dennis Weaver
Don Cheadle	Bonnie Franklin	Jessica Lange	Bonnie Raitt	Bradley Whitford
Jill Clayburgh	John Fugelsang	Tea Leoni	Carl Reiner	James Whitmore
David Clennon	Jeananne Garafalo	Donal Logue	Tim Robbins	James Whitmore, Jr.
Jack Coleman	Larry Gelbart	Wendie Malick	Steve Robinson, Sgt., U.S. Army (Ret.) (National Gulf War Resource Center)	Alfre Woodard
Peter Coyote	Melissa Gilbert	Camryn Manheim		Noah Wyle
Lindsay Crouse	Danny Glover	Marsha Mason		Peter Yarrow
Suzanne Cryer	Elliott Gould	Richard Masur	Mitch Ryan	Howard Zinn

Add Your Name to This Petition. Go to www.moveon.org.

This ad brought to you by:

MoveOn.ORG
Democracy in Action.

TomPaine.common sense
A Public Interest Journal
A Project of
The Florence Fund

www.femtom.com

As Farrell and Greenwald contacted friends and colleagues in the entertainment community, they were "surprised, amazed and thrilled" at the positive response.[10] More than one hundred entertainers signed the Artists United statement, which was modeled on the statement of the Win Without War coalition. The artists committee was officially launched on December 10, 2002, with a full-page ad in the *New York Times* and a press event in Los Angeles. More than two dozen artists came to the launch event, including Anjelica Houston, Tony Shalhoub, Loretta Switt, and Martin Sheen. Retired admiral Eugene Carroll, former deputy director of the Center for Defense Information, was on hand to provide expert commentary and validation for the artists' concerns. After the press conference Artists United hired a staff director, former film producer Kate McArdle, who worked with Farrell and Greenwald to recruit additional artists and arrange interviews on news and entertainment programs. Through these efforts Artists United reached an estimated 125 million people with the antiwar message.[11]

The formation of Musicians United to Win Without War came a couple of months later. Former Talking Heads star David Byrne and a few other musicians had signed the artists statement in December. As the likelihood of war increased, Byrne and other musical performers decided to issue their own statement. Byrne contacted David Fenton to help produce an ad and plan the group's public announcement. Fenton raised the idea of a musicians committee in a meeting with producer Russell Simmons.[12] In February Fenton and Tom Andrews met in New York with Simmons, Byrne, and others to form the new group. Musicians United to Win Without War was launched with a full-page ad in the *New York Times* on February 27, 2003 and a New York press event attended by Byrne, Simmons, and other performers. The musicians statement, again modeled on the Win Without War appeal, was signed by fifty of the world's most popular rap, hip-hop, and rock musicians, including Roseanne Cash, Sheryl Crow, Jay-Z, Dave Matthews, Mobb Depp, REM, and Suzanne Vega. The newspaper ad said simply, "War on Iraq is Wrong and We Know It." The announcements of the artists and musicians committees generated widespread broadcast and print news coverage. Stories appeared not only in hard news segments, but in entertainment and style programs. Youth-oriented programs like MTV aired frequent stories about the celebrities and musicians, helping to generate widespread sympathy and support for the antiwar cause.

Musicians United to Win Without War was created too late to make a major difference in the mobilization against war. The public announcement came less than a month before the invasion, and the group was unable to follow-up on its successful launch. The musicians planned a major antiwar concert, but the bombs started falling before an event could be organized. An earlier and more sustained effort to engage the many performers opposed to war might have contributed significantly to building antiwar sentiment, especially among young people.

The antiwar statements of artists and entertainers sparked a fierce backlash on right wing radio stations and in the mainstream media. After the virtual march on Washington in late February 2003, KFI-AM in Los Angeles urged its listeners to "march on Hollywood" by flooding the Win Without War phone lines and computer inbox. The Win Without War office was spammed, the fax machine overflowed with vitriol, and the phone lines were jammed with angry and at times obscene messages. Several of the artists were affected directly. Susan Sarandon was disinvited from a United Way event in Florida, and she and her husband Tim Robbins were barred from the Baseball Hall of Fame, which cancelled a planned celebration of the film "Bull Durham." Sarandon and Robbins were unbowed by the pressure and used the resulting publicity to reiterate their criticism of war and to defend their right of dissent. So many sportswriters and fans criticized the Hall of Fame cancellation that its president had to admit his mistake and Major League Baseball disavowed any connection with the decision. In a speech to the National Press Club, Robbins expressed gratitude for the support he received, which he acknowledged was "not about my views but my right to express them."[13] The controversy brought the debate over war into the sports pages.

The strongest right wing reaction was reserved for the Dixie Chicks. During a March 10 concert in London lead singer Natalie Maines told the audience, "Just so you know, we're ashamed the president of the United States is from Texas." The comment touched off a storm of controversy in the normally conservative world of country music. Maines quickly apologized for her comment about the president, but she did not back off from her questioning of the war. "We support our troops," the group said, but "there is nothing more frightening than the notion of going to war with Iraq and the prospect of all the innocent lives that will be lost."[14] The Clear Channel radio network, with some 1,200 stations, ordered Dixie Chicks music off the air. A South Carolina legislator urged fans to run away from the group's concerts. A caller to a right wing talk show suggested that Maines be strapped to a bomb and dropped over "eye-rack."[15] Some hate groups sponsored bonfires to burn the group's

CDs. The trio refused to be intimidated, however, and strongly defended both their right to speak out and their questioning of the war. The Chicks made light of the criticism, appearing on the cover of *Entertainment Weekly* in a nude pose with slogans on their bodies. They refused to give in when challenged on national television by ABC's Diane Sawyer. Despite the right wing attacks, or perhaps because of them, the Dixie Chicks remained immensely popular. Their hit CD, "Home," picked up sales and climbed to number one on Billboard's country chart, selling more than six million copies. Of the fifty-nine concerts on their U.S. tour in 2003, only six had any seats available, and these were 85 to 90 percent sold.[16] Many artists came to the defense of the Chicks, including Bruce Springsteen who wrote on his website that banishing the group from radio networks was "un-American."[17] When Maines received the VH1 "big quote of the year" award in November 2003, she jokingly thanked "all the haters because you make me strong, empowered, involved and proud." The group's courageous stand strengthened and empowered many of those who spoke out against war.

The participation of celebrities helped the antiwar movement achieve the "publicness" that social change groups must establish to convey their message to the mass media. A famous face or well-known personality can help to overcome media disinterest and draw attention to a message that the political establishment would prefer to ignore or bury. The involvement of celebrities is not without drawbacks, however. An overemphasis on media stars can divert attention from the unglamorous but necessary tasks of grassroots organizing and organization building. A focus on celebrity may also devalue the collective, participatory, behind-the-scenes nature of social activism and nonviolent leadership.[18] Some of these drawbacks were evident during the Iraq antiwar campaign. Media commentators criticized artists for supposedly exploiting their celebrity to speak on a complicated matter of national security. The artists often had to spend time defending their right to speak as citizens. Fenton Communications attempted to pair artists with policy exerts, but talk show producers usually insisted on booking artists alone. Several of the most active artists—including Farrell, Sarandon, and Janeane Garofalo—appeared on numerous television and radio interview programs. They were well-read and informed about the issues and were effective in conveying the Win Without War message.

The Iraq antiwar movement was more successful than previous peace campaigns at media communications. Through extensive use of the Internet, professional public relations services, paid newspaper and television advertising, and the participation of famous artists and musicians, the movement utilized the tools of mass communications to an unprecedented degree. More than a dozen full-page ads in the *New York Times*, hundreds of ads in local newspapers, hundreds of national and regional television ad placements, thousands of national and local television and radio interview appearances, and thousands of articles in national and local newspapers—all brought visibility and credibility to the antiwar message. The Win Without War media effort generated hundreds of millions of viewer impressions. This vast media communications campaign both reflected and shaped public opinion and influenced the political climate in which the Bush administration went to war.

Notes

1. Charlotte Ryan, *Prime Time Activism* (Boston: South End Press), 31–35.

2. William Gamson, *The Strategy of Social Protest*, 2nd ed. (Belmont, Calif.: Wadsworth Publishing, 1990), 147.

3. Lakoff quoted in Robert Salladay, "Peace Activism: A Matter of Language," *San Francisco Chronicle*, 7 April 2003.

4. Salladay, "Peace Activism."

5. The phrase was derived from the report by David Cortright, Alistair Millar, and George A. Lopez, *Winning Without War: Sensible Security Options for Dealing with Iraq*, October 2002, Policy Brief F5, <http://www.fourthfreedom.org/pdf/www_rpt.pdf> (accessed 21 November 2003).

6. See the Gallup poll analysis, <http://www.gallup.com/subscription/?m=f&c_id=13142> (accessed 1 December 2003).

7. Polling Report, "Iraq (p. 4)," <http://www.pollingreport.com/iraq4.htm> (accessed 28 August 2003).

8. Polling Report, "Iraq (p. 4)," conducted by Princeton Survey Research Associates, <http://www.pollingreport.com/iraq4.htm> (accessed 28 August 2003).

9. A February 12-18 poll commissioned by the Program on International Policy Attitudes at the University of Maryland found public support for giving UN inspections more time. When asked if war should be used only after trying to make inspections work, 51 percent said yes, while 45 percent agreed inspections would falter and that it was necessary to invade Iraq.

10. Robert Greenwald, e-mail message to author, 2 December 2003.

11. Greenwald, e-mail message.

12. David Fenton, interview by author, 30 December 2003.

13. Tim Robbins, "A Chill Wind is Blowing in this Nation" (speech, National Press Club, Washington, D.C., 15 April 2003), <http://www.commondreams.org/views03/0416-01.htm> (accessed 21 December 2003).

14. The Dixie Chicks Official Artist Club, "From the Dixie Chicks with Respect to Statements Being Reported in the British Media," 12 March 2003, <http://dixiechicks.launch.yahoo.com/news.asp?id=24> (accessed 16 December 2003).

15. Charles Taylor, "Chicks Against the Machine," *Salon* (28 April 2003), <http://www.salon.com/ent/music/feature/2003/04/28/chicks_sawyer/print.html> (accessed 16 December 2003).

16. CNN, "Chicks Defiant," 24 November 2003, <http://www.cnn.com/2003/SHOWBIZ/Music/04/24/dixie.chicks?> (accessed 16 December 2003).

17. Quoted in CNN, "Chicks Defiant."

18. Brian Martin and Wendy Varney, *Nonviolence Speaks: Communicating Against Repression* (Cresskill, N.J.: Hampton Press, 2003), 157.

Chapter Five

Supporting the Troops

Iraq was not a war that military commanders were anxious to lead or troops eager to fight. Throughout the military community—regular troops, reservists, veterans, and family members—misgivings about attacking Iraq were widespread. As the White House threatened military action, former generals and respected military leaders urged caution. In August 2002 former general Brent Scowcroft, national security adviser for the first president Bush, wrote an article, "Don't Attack Saddam," for the *Wall Street Journal*, warning that an invasion "would seriously jeopardize, if not destroy, the global counterterrorist campaign."[1] In October General Anthony Zinni, former Marine Corps commandant and Middle East negotiator, told a Washington audience, "I'm not convinced we need to do this now . . . I believe that [Saddam] can be deterred and is containable at this moment."[2] General Norman Schwarzkopf, commander of the first Gulf War, told the *Washington Post* in January 2003, "I think it is very important for us to wait and see what inspectors come up with."[3] These skeptical statements from eminent senior officers were indications of deeply felt uncertainty within the ranks.

Within the antiwar movement, veterans played an important role in shaping the movement's message and public image. Veterans for Peace and Veterans for Common Sense were active in both United for Peace and Justice and Win Without War. Veterans for Peace was founded in 1985 by veterans of Vietnam and earlier conflicts. Its membership grew rapidly during the Iraq buildup. Veterans for Common Sense was established in 2002 by veterans of the first Gulf War. The vets also formed their own coalition, Veterans Against the War in Iraq. The veterans were a constant reminder of the costs and trauma of war. They noted, for example, that more than 160,000 veterans have qualified for medical disability payments because of medical conditions and illnesses contracted during their service in the first Gulf War. The veterans groups worked together on "operation dire distress," a project in early April 2003 that included a public forum at American University in Washington and a march to the White House with a petition from three thousand veterans.

Most antiwar groups adopted a "support the troops" position, even as they sharply criticized the president for sending the military into dubious battle. Many groups agreed with mainline veterans organizations and promilitary publications in condemning the administration's plans to cut soldier pay and benefits and reduce medical care for veterans. In July 2003 *Army Times* published an article criticizing the "nickel-and-dime treatment" of troops, as reflected in the administration's proposals to roll back imminent-danger pay and family-separation allowances for low-ranking soldiers.[4] Win Without War and other groups supported lobbying efforts that helped restore these proposed cuts. The antiwar movement thus gave substance and new meaning to the idea of supporting the troops. This was an important breakthrough in positioning the movement as patriotic and mainstream.

Military families also played a role in the antiwar movement. Family members have become an important new constituency in today's volunteer armed forces. A majority of service members are now married. This is a substantial change from the Vietnam era, when relatively few soldiers were married. The prolonged occupation of Iraq directly and adversely affected military families, both active duty and reserve. Some of these families took the lead in demanding an end to the occupation. The concerns of family members coalesced in November 2002 in a new organization, Military Families Speak Out (MFSO), which was founded by Nancy Lessin and Charlie Richardson, parents of an Army linguist. When the group sponsored a televised press conference with Veterans for Common Sense in January, the response was overwhelming. More than two hundred military families joined in just forty-eight hours. Within a year MFSO numbered one thousand families.[5] Many of those who contacted the group were new to the peace movement. Typical was the comment of a wife who confided to Lessin: "Our family has been military for generations. I'm a lifelong Republican. I voted for President Bush. But we've been lied to. I want my husband home."[6] Some family members were concerned only with bringing their own spouse or relative home, with no consideration for the larger mission. Lessin and Richardson tried to help these family members understand the broader policy issues, and to support the call to bring all the troops home. In August 2003 MFSO joined with Veterans for Peace and others to launch a "Bring Them Home Now" campaign. The campaign and the military families' network attracted substantial press coverage.

The demand to bring the troops home was controversial for some antiwar groups, especially in the Win Without War coalition. Antiwar activists had been united in opposing the war before it started, but

Veterans organizations participating in the February 15 rally in New York (photo, Peter Holderness).

once the occupation began and American forces assumed responsibility for Iraq's future, different positions emerged. Groups agreed on the need to end the U.S. occupation, but they had different perspectives on when and how this should occur. Some groups were concerned that a rapid withdrawal of U.S. troops would worsen the chaos in Iraq and abdicate Washington's legal obligations as an occupying power under the Geneva conventions. ANSWER and United for Peace and Justice did not specify the conditions for ending the occupation but simply demanded that the troops come home now. Win Without War adopted a more nuanced position, urging that the U.S. internationalize the political transition in Iraq and begin a gradual troop withdrawal. The differences were slight, between those advocating an immediate pullout and those urging a phased withdrawal, and did not prevent the different coalitions from continuing to work together against Bush administration policy.

During the Vietnam War an organized political opposition developed among active duty soldiers. I was part of that movement, and helped to organize soldier antiwar protests at Fort Hamilton, New York, and Fort Bliss, Texas. Nothing of this sort emerged during the Iraq experience, but there were unmistakable signs of deep misgivings within the ranks. As troops assembled in Kuwait in the early months of 2003, they brought with them the widespread skepticism about war that existed at home. A reporter for the New York *Daily News* who interviewed troops just before the invasion reported that many "would give peace a chance if they had the choice." The war was a troubling matter of conscience for many troops, said a military chaplain. "I've been surprised at how much sympathy there is with the position of the Pope," he told the reporter.[7] The soldiers were willing to perform their duties as ordered, but for many their hearts were not in it.

The war began ominously for the Army. Just three days after the invasion started, an explosion ripped through the headquarters tent of the 101st Airborne Division at Camp Pennsylvania in central Kuwait. The deadly grenade attack killed one officer and wounded a dozen others. The perpetrator was not an Iraqi terrorist but U.S. Army Sgt. Asan Akbar, an engineer from the 326th Engineer Battalion from Fort Campbell, Kentucky. An Army spokesperson said that Sgt. Akbar had "an attitude problem" and was angry about the war.[8] The horrifying incident brought back grim memories of the "fraggings" that shocked the Army in Vietnam. According to Pentagon figures, there were more than five hundred fragging assaults from 1969 through 1971, resulting in more than eighty fatalities, mostly among officers and noncommissioned officers.[9] The Camp Pennsylvania fragging was an isolated incident, but it left many commanders and troops shaken.

After defeating the Iraqi army and conquering Baghdad in just three weeks, American troops hoped for a quick return home. They were led to believe that "the way home is through Baghdad." Instead they were assigned to nation building duty and became bogged down in a prolonged military occupation. When troops were informed during the summer of 2003 that their return home would be delayed, there was a palpable wave of resentment through the ranks and among family members. Soldiers expressed their dissent not through petitions as some of us did during the Vietnam era, but through e-mails and comments to news reporters. Iraq was the first wired war, and many troops had access to the Internet. They communicated with family, friends, and hometown newspapers. Their messages were frank and unabashed, and often expressed widespread doubts about the mission in Iraq. Newspapers reported a flood of "war-weary e-mails."[10] Retired Colonel David Hackworth, a highly-decorated soldier and prolific writer and media commentator, reported receiving five hundred e-mails a day, many from soldiers in Iraq complaining about mistreatment by officers, shoddy equipment, and a flawed mission.[11] Filmmaker Michael Moore reported receiving hundreds of letters from the troops, including this message from a Marine lance corporal: "You'd be surprised at how many of the guys I talked to in my company and others believed that the president's scare about Saddam's WMD was a bunch of bullshit and that the real motivation for this war was only about money."[12] In early July a message circulated on the Internet from soldiers of the Second Brigade, Third Infantry Division, based at Fallujah: "Our morale is not high or even low. Our morale is nonexistent."

Family members were especially angry when military commanders announced that deployments would be extended. At Fort Stewart, Georgia, home of the Third Infantry Division, family frustrations reached the boiling point. In early July the *New York Times* reported an incident in which a colonel, meeting with eight hundred "seething spouses," had to be escorted from the session. The family members were "crying, cussing, yelling, and screaming for their men to come back," according to the director of community services at the base.[13] A couple of weeks later the Fort Stewart wives organized a gathering of nearly one hundred family members in a vacant shopping center near the base to announce a letter writing campaign to bring the troops home.[14] Hundreds of family members subsequently contacted their elected representatives and members of the press.[15] Press accounts told of similar discontent and anger among family members at Fort Gordon, Georgia; Fort Hood, Texas; and Fort Campbell, Kentucky. At Fort Campbell, according to one report, "frustration runs especially high in the treeless blocks of low-rent apartments where many younger soldiers live." Concern about attacks on American troops was "gnawing at support for the U.S. mission."[16]

Some soldiers took their concerns directly to the press. In July national television viewers of ABC's "Good Morning America" heard remarkably blunt comments from soldiers of the Second Brigade, Third Infantry Division: "If Donald Rumsfeld was here I'd ask for his resignation," Specialist Clinton Deitz told an interviewer. "I've got my own 'most wanted' list," said a sergeant. "The aces in my deck are Paul Bremer, Donald Rumsfeld, George Bush, and Paul Wolfowitz." The Pentagon acted swiftly to muzzle such dissent. Commanders announced that soldiers who criticize senior officials in public would be punished. At some bases family members received e-mails admonishing them to refrain from public complaints. At the Third Infantry Division officers feared they would lose their jobs over the ABC incident. Said one, "This thing went all the way up to President Bush and back down on top of us."[17] The Army also tried to manipulate the press, launching a campaign of managed letters home to local newspapers. Identical letters to the editor from different soldiers in the Second Battalion of the 503rd Infantry

Regiment appeared in eleven newspapers across the country, according to a report by Gannett News Service. The letters gave upbeat accounts of American efforts in Iraq and said that U.S. troops were welcomed "with open arms."[18]

Pressure and media manipulation could not alter the deeply felt grievances of service members and their families. Angry e-mail messages continued to pour forth. Many of these were sent to *Stars and Stripes*, a traditional military newspaper that receives some funding from the Pentagon but is not subject to its editorial control. After receiving scores of messages from troops in Iraq, more than half of them complaining, *Stars and Stripes* decided to conduct an in-depth investigation. In August the newspaper sent seven reporters to visit nearly fifty camps in Iraq, interviewing troops and administering an informal questionnaire. Though the findings were unscientific, drawn from 1,935 completed surveys, they showed widespread discontent. Half of those interviewed considered their unit morale low, and more than a third did not consider their mission clearly defined.[19] In the survey, 49 percent described their units' morale as low, with 16 percent calling it high. When asked if they thought the war in Iraq was worthwhile, 31 percent said it was of "little value" or "no value at all." Among Army troops, by far the largest group in Iraq, 36 percent said the mission was not clearly defined. According to the paper's analysis, "last spring's good-natured grousing about lousy food and no showers has given way to edgier complaints about inequality among the forces and lack of confidence in their leaders."[20]

Problems of low morale were greatest among reservists and National Guard members. The mobilization of reserve forces that began with Afghanistan and accelerated for the war in Iraq put an enormous strain on reserve troops and their families. As of November 2003, approximately 42,000 of the 160,000 U.S. troops in the Iraq theatre were members of the Reserves and National Guard.[21] More than 160,000 Reserve and Guard troops were on active duty throughout the military. These troops tended to be older than active duty soldiers, were more likely to be married, and had jobs and professional commitments in their communities. When called to active service, they were separated from family and experienced a significant disruption and reduction in the quality of life. Not surprisingly, they and their families were most vocal in complaining about the mission and demanding a return home. In the *Stars and Stripes* survey, 71 percent of Reservists and Guard members rated their units' morale low or very low. The interviewers found many reservists angry and confused, unsure of their mission, and disappointed in their commanders.[22] Family members shared these frustrations and campaigned publicly for the troops' return.

In Kansas, family members of the 129th Transportation Company of the Army Reserve set up a website and gathered eight thousand signatures on a petition demanding an end to extended duty tours in Iraq. In Florida, twenty National Guard family members petitioned military commanders to bring the troops home. Some of the soldier wives vowed to go on hunger strikes if their demands were not met.[23]

By late 2003 the first signs of overt resistance within the ranks began to appear. In October, thirty soldiers who went home on two-week leave missed their return flight from Baltimore.[24] In Rochester, New York, more than a dozen members of the 401st Civil Affairs Battalion refused to sign waivers for their unit to redeploy to the combat zone.[25] The GI Rights hotline, a national soldiers' support service, reported receiving hundreds of calls a week to their toll free number, many from soldiers or family members asking about the penalties associated with going absent without leave (AWOL).[26] At Fort Bragg, North Carolina, home to the 101st Airborne Division, unauthorized absence rates doubled, rising from 107 in the twelve months before September 2002 to 235 in the twelve months ending September 2003.[27]

Whether these scattered signs of resistance will develop into a full-blown crisis in the ranks depends on how long American forces remain in Iraq and what conditions they face there. If the Pentagon attempts to maintain a large occupation force for a prolonged period, morale problems could worsen, and internal opposition grow. This could have direct bearing on the ability of the Pentagon to sustain the occupation and impose its will on Iraq. The prospects for military opposition will depend in part on the level of support soldiers and their families receive from the larger antiwar movement. Those with the courage to stand up for their rights within the military deserve civilian support. The military community can be an important ally in challenging the use of the armed forces for illegitimate purposes.

Opposing Occupation

The antiwar movement did not end when U.S. troops entered Baghdad. To be sure, many activists experienced profound disappointment when the war began. More than a few of us shed tears. Some turned to prayer and spiritual reflection. All felt anguish at a war that was so obviously unjustified. We grieved for the thousands of people who would die in this needless conflict. But disappointment did not turn to disillusionment. Most activists remained determined to continue working against war and the larger danger of U.S. militarism. I wrote in *The Nation* that, "the outbreak of war makes our work more important and necessary than ever."[28] United for Peace and Justice, Win Without War, and other major coalitions held together and continued to mobilize. The invasion and military occupation of Iraq opened a new phase in the crisis of American policy, and created new challenges for the advocates of justice and peace.

In the immediate aftermath of the invasion, the agenda of the antiwar movement broadened to include a range of concerns:

- *Protecting the Innocent:* Antiwar groups demanded that the United States provide humanitarian assistance and economic aid for the Iraqi people who were victimized by the war. The antiwar movement joined with humanitarian relief organizations in urging that this assistance be administered by civilian agencies, not the Pentagon. Relief groups such as the American Friends Service Committee and Oxfam joined with the National Council of Churches and other faith-based groups to raise funds for direct humanitarian relief. Working Assets and MoveOn raised hundreds of thousands of dollars in emergency relief funds, which were donated to Doctors Without Borders, Mercy Corps, and other humanitarian agencies.

- *Supporting the Troops:* Many groups issued statements expressing respect and gratitude to men and women in uniform. Win Without War joined with Veterans for Peace, Veterans for Common Sense, and other groups to demand full funding for soldier benefits and veterans' medical care. True Majority, Veterans for Common Sense, and Responsible Wealth joined together in publishing a full-page ad in the *New York Times* in May criticizing the administration's proposed cuts in soldiers' and veterans' benefits and social spending reductions that would adversely affect service members and their families.

- *Bringing the Troops Home:* United for Peace and Justice, Not In Our Name, and other coalitions took the lead in demanding an immediate military withdrawal from Iraq and an end to the U.S. occupation. Many of the groups in Win Without War were uncomfortable with this demand and argued instead for a more gradual withdrawal of U.S. forces, with the international community taking responsibility for managing the political transition in Iraq and providing security. All the groups were united in opposing any Pentagon plans to create long-term or permanent military bases in Iraq.

- *Opposing Threats to Iran and Other Countries:* Within days of the fall of Baghdad, hard-liners in the Bush administration began making threats against Iran and Syria. It was no secret that extremists in Washington and Israel favored military strikes against Iran as the next phase in the "war on terror." Movement leaders opposed any attempt to coerce or threaten Iran or other countries in the region, warning that further military attacks could have catastrophic consequences.

- *Monitoring the Occupation:* "No war for oil" was a common slogan at antiwar rallies before the invasion. The administration insisted that oil had nothing to do with the U.S. interest in Iraq, but many suspected otherwise. Sure enough, as soon as U.S. forces took over Baghdad, they asserted control over Iraqi oil revenues. In May the UN Security Council adopted a resolution lifting economic sanctions on Iraq and giving the U.S. occupation command exclusive authority to spend Iraqi oil revenues.[29] The occupation authority also ordered the privatization of the Iraqi economy and used the reconstruction process to award no-bid contracts to politically connected firms such as Halliburton, where Vice President Dick Cheney had been chief executive. Antiwar groups criticized U.S. control of Iraqi oil revenues and demanded that the management of these resources be left to the Iraqi people. Global Exchange and United for Peace and Justice created a new group, Occupation Watch, to expose corruption and cronyism in the awarding of contracts for Iraq's reconstruction.

- *Supporting Middle East Peace:* Many activists opposed both the U.S. occupation of Iraq and the Israeli occupation of Palestine. They criticized the Bush administration for its support of the Sharon government and its unwillingness to work for an equitable and just peace settlement between Israel and Palestine. Some groups also called for regional disarmament, recalling that the original 1991 Gulf War cease-fire resolution specified that the disarmament of Iraq was to be the first step toward the creation in the Middle East of a "zone free from weapons of mass destruction."[30] The elimination of weapons of mass destruction in Iraq, they argued, should lead to their elimination in Israel and throughout the region.

In June 2003, United for Peace and Justice held a successful national strategy conference in Chicago. More than 550 people from thirty-eight states, representing 325 local and national groups, participated in the gathering. The conference was at times unwieldy and raucous, as the delegates considered eighty-seven action proposals, decided on a new leadership structure, and elected a racially diverse steering committee to guide the coalition. But the participants showed remarkable discipline and dedication in deciding on a common program to continue the coalition's work. The conference winnowed the many action proposals into an overall strategic framework, and then through a series of intensive workshops and forums prioritized a number of action campaigns. These included:

- Opposing the Bush administration's doctrine of preemptive war and empire;

- Opposing the U.S. military occupation of Iraq;

- Opposing attacks on immigrants and civil liberties in the United States;

- Linking the antiwar movement to the campaign for global justice and mobilizing against the World Trade Organization and the Free Trade Area of the Americas;

- Working for a peaceful end to the Israeli occupation of Palestinian territories; and

- Working for global nuclear disarmament and opposing U.S. efforts to develop new, more useable nuclear weapons.

United for Peace and Justice continued to emphasize street protests and demonstrations as its primary means of conveying the antiwar message. The coalition agreed to partner with ANSWER in sponsoring demonstrations against the U.S. occupation on October 25, 2003. Tens of thousands of people gathered in Washington, D.C., San Francisco, and other cities that day to call for an end to the occupation and for U.S. troops to return home. Speakers at the rallies condemned the Patriot Act, the crackdown on civil liberties at home, and the huge financial costs of the war.[31] United for Peace and Justice also participated in the protests against the Free Trade Area of the Americas ministerial meeting in Miami in November 2003. United for Peace and Justice worked to highlight the links between corporate globalization and war, and build bridges between the global justice and peace movements. United for Peace and Justice also worked with the Win Without War coalition and other groups in opposing the administration's $87 billion budget request for continuing the occupation in Iraq and Afghanistan. Through these and other actions United for Peace and Justice continued to press a broad antiwar agenda that combined concerns for social justice and freedom at home with opposition to war abroad. In so doing, the coalition sought to build a new kind of peace movement, more diverse in membership and methods, and dedicated to a fundamental change in U.S. foreign and domestic policy.

Win Without War also maintained an active program in the months after the invasion. Most of the member groups gathered for a planning retreat at the Omega Institute, an hour north of New York City, in late April 2003. The coalition decided on a three-part program for the future: an educational project on foreign policy alternatives, a nonpartisan voter engagement program, and opposition to the U.S. military occupation of Iraq:

- *Real Security:* The coalition agreed to challenge the Bush doctrine of preemptive unilateralism by promoting cooperative security strategies as more effective means of countering terrorism and weapons proliferation. Peace Action launched a Campaign for a New U.S. Foreign Policy, Physicians for Social Responsibility developed a "real security" program, and the Fourth Freedom Forum and the Kroc Institute at Notre Dame produced a policy report, *Toward a More Secure America*, that was endorsed by twenty former national security and foreign policy officials. These materials were disseminated widely as part of a broad public educational effort to build support for alternatives to the Bush doctrine.

- *Voter Education:* Win Without War sponsored ongoing media efforts to remind voters of the Bush administration's deceptions in justifying the war. The goal was to prevent the Bush administration from using the war issue to rally public support for the president's reelection. The coalition constantly emphasized the administration's deceit as a way of undermining voter confidence in the president's leadership.

- *Opposing U.S. Occupation:* The coalition called for internationalizing the transition process in Iraq and the phased withdrawal of U.S. forces. The Education for Peace in Iraq Center, the Fourth Freedom Forum, and other groups developed position papers urging the U.S. to turn over authority to the

United Nations and accelerate the creation of a transitional government in Iraq with full sovereign powers.

Win Without War continued to emphasize media communications and Internet-based organizing as its principal modes of action. MoveOn, True Majority, and Working Assets remained the most active members of the coalition and took the lead in mobilizing political opposition to Bush administration policies. MoveOn raised millions of dollars from its online membership for a series of hard-hitting ads blasting administration policies. In June MoveOn and Win Without War published a *New York Times* ad labeling the president a "misleader." The ad called for an independent investigation of the administration for misleading the country into war. The misleader ad was the opening salvo in a campaign to hold the administration accountable for its deceptions. The public response to the ad was enthusiastic, generating more than one hundred thousand messages to Congress in the first twenty-four hours. MoveOn also produced television ads that were aired in dozens of communities around the United States. The misleader concept was so popular that MoveOn created a new website, "misleader.org." MoveOn commissioned Robert Greenwald to produce a documentary film, *Uncovered*, which relied upon interviews with former national security officials to rebut the administration's justifications for war. MoveOn sold forty thousand copies of the documentary and in December organized more than 2,800 house parties at which one hundred thousand people watched the film.[32]

MoveOn and Win Without War continued to press the misleader theme, launching a second wave of ads in July and promoting media appearances by national director Tom Andrews. As the second round of misleader ads hit the newspapers and the air waves, member groups organized simultaneous press events in local communities. The American Friends Service Committee, Physicians for Social Responsibility, Women's Action for New Directions (WAND), and other groups sponsored appearances by local leaders to demand an independent investigation of the administration's deceptions and misuse of intelligence data. Events took place in dozens of cities, including Chicago, Des Moines, Philadelphia, Pittsburgh, Milwaukee, Little Rock, Phoenix, and Seattle. The ads and local events generated another surge of grassroots pressure, with MoveOn reporting that 400,000 messages were sent to Congress. The groups supported proposals by Representatives Henry Waxman (D-CA) and Ellen Tauscher (D-CA) for a congressionally mandated inquiry into the administration's deceptions.[33] In August True Majority and Working Assets joined with WAND, MoveOn, and other groups to organize

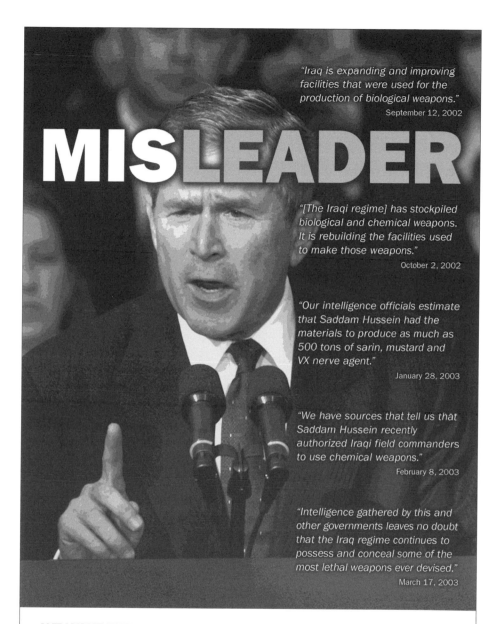

"Iraq is expanding and improving facilities that were used for the production of biological weapons."
September 12, 2002

MISLEADER

"[The Iraqi regime] has stockpiled biological and chemical weapons. It is rebuilding the facilities used to make those weapons."
October 2, 2002

"Our intelligence officials estimate that Saddam Hussein had the materials to produce as much as 500 tons of sarin, mustard and VX nerve agent."
January 28, 2003

"We have sources that tell us that Saddam Hussein recently authorized Iraqi field commanders to use chemical weapons."
February 8, 2003

"Intelligence gathered by this and other governments leaves no doubt that the Iraq regime continues to possess and conceal some of the most lethal weapons ever devised."
March 17, 2003

WE WANT THE TRUTH NOW.

America rallied around a President who warned of the imminent danger of weapons of mass destruction, who promised the evidence for such weapons was incontrovertible. Now, months later, no weapons have been found. Worse, the evidence suggests that intelligence reports were deliberately misread, that the American people were deliberately misled. It would be a tragedy if young men and women were sent to die for a lie.

☐ YES! I want the truth.
Your contribution will help fund additional efforts to tell the real story behind the headlines.

NAME

ADDRESS

CITY   STATE   ZIP

E-MAIL ADDRESS

Make checks payable to MoveOn.org. Mail to MoveOn.org, 336 Bon Air Center #354, Greenbrae, CA 94904. Contributions to MoveOn.org are not tax deductible.

MoveOn.org Win Without War

CALL YOUR REPRESENTATIVE AND SENATORS NOW AND DEMAND AN INDEPENDENT COMMISSION TO DETERMINE THE TRUTH.

coordinated local meetings with key members of Congress in their home districts. More than one thousand activists visited the local offices of fifty-seven members of the House of Representatives and five senators in late August. United for Peace and Justice participated in this grassroots lobbying effort. The constituent pressure generated by these efforts produced dozens of additional congressional sponsors for the Waxman and Tauscher measures, but Republican congressional leaders continued to stonewall and refused to permit an independent investigation.

The movement's media and mobilizing efforts came in the context of constant press revelations about the failure to discover weapons of mass destruction in Iraq. The combination of the movement's media efforts and the press reports helped to erode public confidence in the administration's credibility. Polling data from CBS and Gallup surveys during the summer showed that the public was starting to have doubts about the president's justifications and began to question the value of the war. The Gallup organization reported in late July that "the rally effect that President George W. Bush enjoyed among the American public in the wake of the Iraq war has essentially disappeared." The president's overall job approval and his ratings on the handling of foreign affairs and the situation in Iraq fell back to levels measured prior to the war.[34] A late September poll by the *New York Times* and CBS found that "the public's confidence in President Bush's ability to deal wisely with an international crisis has slid over the past five months."[35] The poll found that for the first time Americans were more critical than not of the president's ability to handle foreign affairs.

In the fall of 2003 the focus of attention for antiwar groups became the Bush administration's $87 billion funding request for the military occupation and reconstruction of Iraq and operations in Afghanistan. True Majority launched a "no blank check" campaign against the funding request. Win Without War demanded that the administration "change the course and change the team" before receiving additional funding. MoveOn circulated a petition urging Congress to withhold the $87 billion until President Bush dismissed the team responsible for the Iraq quagmire, starting with Defense Secretary Rumsfeld. In the weeks before the October vote on the funding request, True Majority, Working Assets, and MoveOn generated more than 325,000 calls, letters, and e-mails to members of Congress.[36] Despite this grassroots pressure, and opinion polls showing public opposition to the $87 billion appropriation, Congress overwhelmingly approved the measure. Even members of Congress who had opposed the October 2002 war resolution voted in favor of the funding request, in large part to show their support for the troops. It was not realistic to expect that Congress would vote against funding for U.S. military forces facing hostile fire in the field. Yet antiwar groups felt they could not simply remain silent about such a huge funding request. Win Without War attempted to find a middle ground by calling on Congress to use its power of the purse to mandate a more international transition process in Iraq, but few congressional leaders were willing to support this or any other challenge to the funding request.

As the year 2003 came to a close, the antiwar movement faced frustrating paradoxes. On the one hand, the movement remained active, with the major coalitions continuing to sponsor significant protest actions, media campaigns, and grassroots lobbying efforts. Hundreds of thousands of activists remained engaged and continued to protest, sign petitions, lobby members of Congress, attend meetings, and contribute money. Yet a palpable Iraq war fatigue began to set in. Activists tired of the relentlessly depressing news from Baghdad, the constant deception and denial of reality from officials in Washington, and their own inability to steer the U.S. government away from the deepening morass in Iraq. Increasingly the attention of activists turned toward the 2004 national elections, in the hope that they could vote the war makers out of office and turn the country away from militarism toward peace and international cooperation.

Notes

1. Brent Scowcroft, "Don't Attack Saddam," *Wall Street Journal*, 15 August 2002.

2. General Anthony Zinni, (speech, Middle East Institute annual conference, Washington, D.C., 19 October 2002), <http://www.novaserve.ns.ca/html/article623.html> (accessed 11 December 2003).

3. Thomas E. Ricks, "Desert Caution," *Washington Post*, 28 January 2003, C1.

4. Chuck Vinch, "Republicans Praise Troops, but Neglect Fiscal Support," *Army Times*, 18 July 2003.

5. Nancy Lessin and Charlie Richardson, interview by author, 20 December 2003.

6. Lessin and Richardson, interview.

7. Richard Sisk, "Uneasy GIs Speak Their Peace," *Daily News* (New York), 16 March 2003, 4.

8. Oliver Burkeman, "War in the Gulf: One Killed, Twelve Injured by 'Resentful' Muslim GI," *The Guardian* (London), 24 March 2003, 6.

9. See the author's account in *Soldiers in Revolt: The American Military Today* (New York: Anchor Press/Doubleday, 1975), 44.

10. Paul Harris and Jonathan Franklin, "Bring us Home: GIs Flood U.S. with War-Weary Emails," *The Guardian* (London), 10 August 2003, <http://www.guardian.co.uk/print/0,3858,4730213-103550,00.html> (accessed 11 December 2003).

11. Harris and Franklin, "Bring us Home."

12. Michael Moore, "Letters the Troops Have Sent Me," 19 December 2003, <http://www.michaelmoore.com> (accessed 20 December 2003).

13. Jeffrey Gettleman, "Anger Rises for Families of Troops in Iraq," *New York Times*, 4 July 2003, A1.

14. Noelle Phillips, "Some Fort Stewart Wives Grow Bitter as Deployment Continues," *Savannah Morning News*, 14 July 2003, <http://www.savannahnow.com/stories/071403/LOCtroopdelay.shtml> (accessed 11 December 2003).

15. Noelle Phillips, "The Long Road Home," *Savannah Morning News*, 20 July 2003, <http://www.savannahnow.com/stories/072003/LOCtroopreturn.shtml> (accessed 11 December 2003).

16. Wes Allison, "A Moment to Remember Fallen Comrades; In a Soldiers' Haven, Worry and Frustration Taking a Toll," *St. Petersburg Times*, 7 November 2003, 1A.

17. Robert Collier, "Pentagon Retaliates Against GIs who Spoke out on TV," *San Francisco Chronicle*, 18 July 2003, A1.

18. Dana Milbank, "Bush Courts Regional Media," *Washington Post*, 14 October 2003, A4.

19. The results of the investigation and questionnaire findings were published in seven consecutive issues of *Stars and Stripes* beginning 15 October 2003, <http://www.stripes.com/morale/> (accessed 11 December 2003).

20. Steve Liewer, "What Will Spell Success?" *Stars and Stripes*, 21 October 2003, 3.

21. David Josar, "From Weekend Warrior to Full-time Fighter," *Stars and Stripes*, 18 October 2003, 5.

22. Josar, "From Weekend Warrior."

23. Vernon Loeb, "Protests Grow Over Yearlong Army Tours," *Washington Post*, 20 September 2003, A13.

24. Steve Vogel, "Soldiers Miss Flights Back to Iraq," *Washington Post*, 21 October 2003, A20.

25. Reported in *GI Special* #143, 30 November 2003, <http://www.notinourname.net/gi-special/146.pdf> (accessed 11 December 2003).

26. Leonard Greene, "AWOL State of Mind: Calls From Soldiers Desperate to Leave Iraq Flood Hotline," *New York Post*, 5 October 2003, 12.

27. As reported by Holly Hickman, "Desertions, AWOLs Increase; Officer Admits There is an 'Underground Movement'," *GI Special* #143, 26 November 2003, <http://www.notinourname.net/gi-special/143.pdf> (accessed 11 December 2003).

28. See the author's article, "What We Do Now: A Peace Agenda," *The Nation* (21 April 2003), <http://www.thenation.com/doc.mhtml?i=20030421&s=cortright> (accessed 18 December 2003).

29. See the author's commentary "Oil Spoils," *The Nation* 276, no. 23 (16 June 2003): 4.

30. United Nations Security Council, *Security Council Resolution 687 (1991)*, S/RES/687, New York, 3 April 1991, para. 14.

31. Manny Fernandez, "In DC, a Diverse Mix Rouses War Protest," *Washington Post*, 26 October 2003, A8.

32. Kate McArdle, interview by Linda Gerber, 8 January 2004.

33. Evelyn Nieves, "Antiwar War Groups Say Public Ire Over Iraq Claims is Increasing," *Washington Post*, 22 July 2003, A3.

34. The Gallup Organization, "Iraq War Rally Effect has Disappeared," 22 July 2003, <http://www.gallup.com/subscription/?m=f+c_id=13711> (accessed 15 December 2003).

35. Todd S. Purdum and Janet Elder, "Poll Shows Drop in Confidence on Bush Skill in Handling Crises," *New York Times*, 3 October 2003, A1.

36. Eli Pariser, e-mail message to Win Without War steering committee, 21 October 2003.

Chapter Six

Reflections

Despite the unprecedented scale and scope of the Iraq antiwar movement—the largest antiwar demonstrations in history, a campaign of global dimensions, a sophisticated and wide-reaching media effort—the Bush administration largely ignored the pervasive opposition to war and rolled ahead with its planned invasion. Given the administration's determination to remove Saddam Hussein by force, the movement probably had little chance of halting the march to war. Nor did the movement have much time to organize, less than six months from when the major coalitions began to take shape in October until the onset of war in March. By the time United for Peace and Justice and Win Without War actually set up shop, war was less than three months away. That the movement was able to do so much in such a short period was testament to the intensity and breadth of popular opposition. As Leslie Cagan observed, it's not that we were such good organizers, but that people were outraged by what the government was doing and had to register their disagreement. We simply gave them the opportunity. That's what happens during a genuine mass movement. People come forward in unexpectedly large numbers, giving freely of their time, money, and effort to express an urgently felt popular conviction. They break out of their isolation and connect with others in an emotionally charged recognition of mutual passion and commitment.[1] The Iraq movement was an exhilarating example of this extraordinary social phenomenon.

This vast antiwar outpouring was not sufficient to sway the unlistening White House, but it nonetheless had significant political impacts. The administration's decision to take its case to the United Nations was a victory for those who advocated the rule of law and the use of diplomacy. By pressuring the White House to go through the UN, the movement slowed the march to war and complicated the administration's military preparations and planning for occupation. Hard-liners in the administration would have preferred bypassing the Security Council and proceeding directly to military action, but the administration needed at least the appearance of seeking UN involvement to gain political legitimacy in Congress and elsewhere. Once the UN debate began, France,

Russia, and other members of the Security Council were successful in forcing substantial changes in the first draft resolution submitted by the U.S. and U.K. in October. The resulting resolution in November, Security Council Resolution 1441, lacked the explicit authorization for military action that Washington and London had sought.

When the Bush administration returned to the Security Council in February and March to seek authority for war, it was decisively rebuffed. Not only France, Germany, and Russia, but also six nonpermanent members—Chile, Mexico, Cameroon, Guinea, Angola, and Pakistan— refused to support the U.S. proposal. The opposition of the nonpermanent members was especially significant, given their political and economic dependence on the United States. Washington made determined efforts to twist arms, including diplomatic missions to each country, but to no avail. Despite its lobbying effort the United States could only count on the votes of Britain, Spain, and Bulgaria. Rather than face the embarrassment of such a meager showing, Washington withdrew its proposed resolution. This was a major victory for the global antiwar movement. The strength of worldwide opposition prevented the Bush administration from gaining Security Council support for its planned invasion and forced the administration to abandon efforts to win UN endorsement.[2] As a result, the United States and Britain stood practically alone in their drive for war. The importance of this Security Council rebuff to the United States is enormous. It was, according to scholar Immanuel Wallerstein, "the first time since the United Nations was founded that the United States, on an issue that mattered to it, could not get a majority on the Security Council."[3] This was widely recognized as a humiliating political defeat for the supposed lone superpower. It represented a major loss of legitimacy and weakening of U.S. political prestige.

The interplay between the antiwar movement and the United Nations deserves special comment. Most UN officials and Security Council members were opposed to the war but were powerless to stop it. The UN Security Council by its very design is a captive of the permanent powers, and when its most powerful member is bent on military aggression, the UN has no capacity to prevent it. The most important power of the Security Council is its authority to confer international legitimacy. When it withholds consent, as it did in Iraq, it denies legitimacy. It was able to do so because of the worldwide antiwar movement. A creative dialectic developed between the Security Council and global civil society. The public opposition to war hinged on the lack of UN authorization. The objection of the UN in turn depended on the strength of antiwar opposition. The stronger the antiwar movement in the United States, Germany, France, Mexico, and other countries, the greater the determination of UN diplomats to resist Bush administration pressures. The stronger the objections at the UN, the greater the legitimacy and political impact of the antiwar movement.[4] It was a unique and unprecedented form of global political synergy. By defending the UN, despite its many shortcomings, and insisting upon international authorization for the use of force, the peace movement helped to build the domestic opposition to war and strengthened respect for international law.

The Bush administration seemed to display an almost indecent haste to commence military action, despite concessions from Saddam Hussein, the progress of UN inspections, and feverish diplomatic efforts at the UN. The attempts of officials from France, Russia, and other countries to broker agreements that would have allowed more time for inspections and diplomacy were brusquely swept aside. A compromise Security Council resolution emerged in March that would have established specific benchmarks and a thirty-day timeline for Iraqi compliance. The Canadian-initiated proposal had the support of ten Security Council members and could have passed, but the Bush administration refused to yield.[5] Instead the White House offered a one-week extension and proceeded with its planned invasion. The administration's calendar for war was dictated in part by the pace of the military buildup, which was largely completed by February. The calendar was also influenced by considerations of weather, and the desire to launch and complete the invasion before the onset of the extreme heat of Iraq's summer. The timing of the attack was also influenced by politics. The administration planned the buildup for war to coincide with the congressional midterm election campaigns, thereby rallying the flag for Republican candidates and distracting attention from Democratic criticisms of the administration's domestic policies. The administration also wanted to complete the war before the presidential election season of 2004, in the hope that it could use the military victory over Iraq's bedraggled army and supposed success in liberating Iraq to bolster the president's campaign.[6]

The administration's haste may have been motivated as well by a desire to launch the attack before antiwar sentiment became too strong. The administration had already made its best case for war (the president's State of the Union address and the Powell presentation at the UN), which produced a bump in the polls as expected. But the short-term gain for the administration in the polls was trumped by the rising tide of antiwar action, particularly the February 15 rallies and the virtual march. In late

February and early March, polls showed a slight decline in support for war, with many opposed to an invasion without Security Council approval, and majority support for giving UN inspections more time. Antiwar momentum was building. Time seemed to be on the side of the opposition. Membership lists were growing rapidly at MoveOn, True Majority, Peace Action, and other groups. Plans were being laid for additional rallies, concerts, and television broadcasts. The best way to short-circuit the antiwar buildup was to send in the troops, thus robbing the movement of its principal purpose and sparking the inevitable rally-around-the-flag effect that occurs when troops are engaged in combat.

The degree to which antiwar opposition affected the deliberations of the Bush administration is unknown, and may not be known until former officials write their memoirs. In the aftermath of the February 15 demonstrations the president professed to be unmoved by the massive protests, saying that he would not decide policy merely on the basis of a "focus group."[7] Such denials of social movement influence are standard fare among political leaders who are the target of protest. During the Vietnam era, President Nixon dismissed the huge Moratorium rally at the Washington Monument on November 15, 1969, claiming that he ignored the protest and was watching football on television. As Daniel Ellsberg later observed, however, the memoirs of Nixon and of his top aide H.R. Halderman showed that the administration was deeply concerned about the Moratorium actions, and was forced to abandon its plans for a major military escalation against North Vietnam for fear of sparking even greater protests.[8] Ronald Reagan and his advisers dismissed the nuclear freeze demonstrations and referenda of the early 1980s as "all sponsored by a thing called the World Peace Council"[9] (a false and absurd attempt to redbait the movement). In fact, public pressure during the 1980s derailed the MX missile system, blocked civil defense planning, persuaded Congress to halt funding for nuclear tests, and forced the White House to begin negotiations with the Soviets that eventually led to significant arms reduction.[10]

One impact of the Iraq antiwar debate that has not been widely acknowledged was the strategic decision of the White House to justify its preplanned war by emphasizing the supposed threat from Iraqi weapons of mass destruction. In a rare moment of unscripted candor after the war, Deputy Defense Secretary Paul Wolfowitz acknowledged that the focus on weapons of mass destruction was politically motivated. During an interview with *Vanity Fair* magazine, Wolfowitz stated: "The truth is that for reasons that have a lot to do with U.S. government bureaucracy, we settled on the one issue that everyone could agree on, which was weapons of mass destruction as the core reason."[11] This was an admission that the administration could not make an honest case for war and win the debate. Because opposition to war was so great, it was necessary to manipulate and deceive public opinion. By choosing to emphasize the weapons threat—invoking fears of a nuclear mushroom cloud and chemical or biological attack—the administration focused the debate on issues it knew would be effective in mobilizing public concern. The tactic was successful in the short term, convincing many Americans that Saddam Hussein had deadly weapons poised to strike. But the strategy backfired when White House claims were exposed as lies—in large part through the continuing efforts of antiwar groups.

The political context of the decision to go to war also had an impact on the failure to plan for the postwar occupation, and the subsequent quagmire in which the United States found itself. The lack of preparation for the aftermath of war (no police on the streets, no public services, no one to manage government ministries) has been widely criticized, but few have linked this failure to the prewar political debate. In the crucial months leading up to the invasion the administration was claiming that it hoped to avoid war. The declared U.S. objective was Iraqi disarmament, not armed regime change. If the planning for a U.S. takeover of Iraq had been more blatant and visible, diplomatic efforts to win support for American policy would have collapsed altogether. Members of Congress would have been more reluctant to issue a blank check for military action. Perhaps even the Blair government in London might have balked. The public opposition to war would have been even greater. To avoid such political resistance, the administration had to maintain the façade of a multilateral disarmament effort, and could not be seen as preparing to take over the Iraqi state. An American official who was involved in the planning for occupation told the *New Yorker*, "That's the political logic that works against advance planning."[12] To maintain the deceit that was necessary to justify military action, the administration short-circuited preparations for the war's aftermath.

It is too early to tell as of this writing how the crisis over the Bush administration's invasion and occupation of Iraq will unfold. The U.S. military easily defeated the overmatched Iraqi armed forces, but the challenge of occupying and controlling Iraq turned out to be far more difficult. Iraq degenerated into violence and chaos, and U.S. and international forces sustained continuing casualties. Many of the arguments made by the opponents of war were proven correct in its aftermath. The supposed Iraqi weapons threat proved to be nonexistent. No evidence was found linking Saddam Hussein with Al Qaeda or the September 11 attacks. Postwar criticisms of faulty and manipulated intelligence undermined confidence in the administration's foreign policy, especially its new doctrine of military preemption, which depends on reliable information about potential threats. As the credibility of U.S. assertions declined and the military's capability to act elsewhere diminished, the administration's doctrine of military preemption suffered a well-deserved setback. The growing awareness that the White House misled the country into war weakened the president's political standing and emboldened his opponents in the Democratic party. The antiwar movement thus continued to have political influence even after the conflict was over.

The ways in which social movements influence policy are not always readily apparent. They often emerge in unanticipated form, or have impacts far into the future. "It is always too early to calculate effect," Rebecca Solnit observed.[13] We can never know today how our actions may influence events tomorrow. Movements can win even as they appear to lose. While the antiwar movement did not succeed in preventing the invasion of Iraq, it helped to set the terms of the debate and exerted decisive influence on public opinion. The Bush administration rammed through its war policy, but it was unable to win the larger and more important struggle for hearts and minds. The White House lost the war politically before it ever began militarily. War is never solely about military results, said Clausewitz, but is an extension of politics, a means of realizing specific political aims. For the Bush administration the war was intended to counter terrorism, validate a new doctrine of unilateral preemption, and extend U.S. domination over the oil-rich Middle East. It was also a cynical effort to boost the president's political standing. In all these areas the war was a failure. It increased rather than decreased the terrorist threat. It demonstrated the folly of preemptive war fought without international support. It overburdened the U.S. military and weakened its capacity to act in other arenas. The international legitimacy of American leadership declined. The Bush administration also suffered political setbacks domestically, as the burdens of occupation and the lack of prohibited weapons exposed the deceit of its case for war. Whether these developments will translate into a long-term loss for U.S. militarism, and a concurrent increase in support for cooperative internationalism, is unknown. The answer will depend on whether the historic legacy of the international movement against war in Iraq is sustained and deepened in the years ahead.

Notes

1. Susan Shaer, interview by author, 14 November 2003.

2. Phyllis Bennis, "Bush Isolated, Launches Terrifying Attack," *War Times,* 9 April 2003, <http://www.war-times.org/issues/9art1.html> (accessed 24 November 2003).

3. Immanuel Wallerstein, "U.S. Weakness and the Struggle for Hegemony," *Monthly Review* 55, no. 3 (July-August 2003): 28.

4. I am indebted for this insight to Jack Odell, interview by author, 17 December 2003.

5. See the analysis by James P. Rubin, "Stumbling into War," *Foreign Affairs* 82, no. 5 (September/October 2003): 56.

6. See the author's commentary on the political planning for war in "Stop the War Before It Starts," *The Progressive* 66, no. 8 (August 2002): 19.

7. Quoted in Richard W. Stevenson, "Antiwar Protests Fail to Sway Bush on Plans for Iraq," *New York Times*, 19 February 2003, A1.

8. See the account of Daniel Ellsberg, "Introduction: A Call to Mutiny," in *Protest and Survive*, eds., E.P. Thompson and Dan Smith (New York: Monthly Review Press, 1981), xv–xvi.

9. Quoted in Strobe Talbott, *Deadly Gambits: The Reagan Administration and the Stalemate in Nuclear Arms Control* (New York: Vintage Books, 1985), 81.

10. See the summary of these impacts by the author in *Peace Works: The Citizen's Role in Ending the Cold War* (Boulder, Colo.: Westview Press, 1993), 243–48.

11. See the transcript of the Wolfowitz interview by Sam Tannenhaus of *Vanity Fair*, 9 May 2003, <http://www.defenselink.mil/transcripts/2003/tr20030509-depsecdef0223.html> (accessed 24 November 2003).

12. George Packer, "War After the War," *New Yorker* (24 November 2003): 64.

13. Rebecca Solnit, "Acts of Hope: Challenging Empire on the World Stage," *Orion* (20 May 2003), <http://www.oriononline.org/pages/oo/sidebars/Patriotism/index_SolnitPR.html> (accessed 24 November 2003).

Appendix

Interviewees

Leslie Cagan—Co-chair, United for Peace and Justice

Steve Cobble—former political director of the National Rainbow Coalition and speechwriter for Rev. Jesse Jackson, Sr.

Melissa Daar—State Political Manager, Working Assets

Reverend Dr. Robert W. Edgar—General Secretary, National Council of Churches

Lynn Erskine—Campaign Coordinator, Win Without War

David Fast—Administrative Assistant and Organizer, Michiana Peace and Justice Collaborative

David Fenton—Chairman, Fenton Communications; co-founder, New Economy Communications

Gary Ferdman—Executive Director, Business Leaders for Sensible Priorities

Bill Fletcher, Jr.—President, TransAfrica Forum; co-chair, United for Peace and Justice

Robert Greenwald—Co-chair, Artists United to Win Without War; Producer/Director, *Uncovered: The Whole Truth About the Iraq War*

Karen Jacob—Chapter President, WAND of Northern Indiana

Nancy Lessin—Co-founder, Military Families Speak Out

Kevin Martin—Executive Director, Peace Action

Kate McArdle—Executive Director, Artists United to Win Without War

Bob Musil—Executive Director, Physicians for Social Responsibility

Jack ODell—Veteran organizer of the Civil Rights Movement; antiwar activist

Eli Pariser—International Campaigns Director, MoveOn

Gerard Powers—Director, Office of International Justice and Peace, United States Conference of Catholic Bishops

Charlie Richardson—Co-founder, Military Families Speak Out

Susan Shaer—Executive Director, WAND

Bob Wing—Editor, *War Times*; founder of *ColorLines*

Mike Yarrow—Organizer, Western Washington Fellowship of Reconciliation, SNOW Coalition